The
Unforgettable
Sermon

How to Write and Deliver Homilies
That Change People's Lives

ED REYNOLDS

Beyond the Rail
PRESS

Revised Standard Version of the Bible, copyright 1952 (2nd edition, 1971) by the Division of Christian Education of the National Council of the Churches of Christ in the United States of America. Used by permission. All rights reserved.

ISBN: 978-0-692-01914-6

Cover photo detail: Rose window in Notre-Dame de Paris © Shutterstock / P.Burghardt

Cover & Interior Design by Scribe Freelance ! www.scribefreelance.com

Published in the United States of America

Contents

"The secret of a good sermon is to have a good beginning and a good ending, then having the two as close together as possible."

—George Burns

Preface

My father was born in the Bronx, New York City, and when it was time for him to learn to swim, his friends took him to the East River. They walked him to the end of a pier and threw him in. It was the "Sink or Swim" school of swimming.

Looking back to my seminary days, I remember my four years of homiletics as a "Sink or Swim" school of preaching. A topic and date were assigned to me and I was then on my own. Feedback came from my classmates who were careful not to bruise my feelings. In the parish, feedback was the occasional "Thank you for your sermon" which was a message in itself. I wasn't very good, sometimes even awful, and didn't know what I had to do to become a good preacher.

Since then, I have taught courses in public speaking, communications, and writing and have sat in the pews for forty years in many different parishes. During those years, I have watched and listened to preachers who I knew were faith filled and dedicated. Some delivered excellent sermons, some mediocre, and some delivered dull and lifeless efforts. All of them wanted to preach well, had prayerfully read the scriptures, and prepared their sermons. Why then did some succeed and others fail?

The answer, I believe, is that in addition to the scriptural and spiritual content of a sermon, a preacher must also learn the techniques and skills of writing and delivering a sermon. These techniques and skills have been well documented in books on writing and public speaking. I have adapted them to fit your needs as a preacher and have added a few more from my own journey. This is a "how to" book about what you need to know to write and deliver sermons and about the "catalysts" that will lift your sermons to life-changing experiences. By mastering them and making them your own, you can become an inspiring preacher.

Introduction

The Unforgettable Sermon

"I've learned that people will forget what you said, people will forget what you did, but people will never forget how you made them feel."
—Maya Angelou

If you preach or hope to preach, I suggest you copy Angelou's sentence and tape it on the wall over the desk where you write your sermons. It will remind you of what you must do to create unforgettable sermons.

Angelou's insight reminds us of an obvious but often neglected truth: The people who listen to preaching are a mix of intellect and emotion, understanding and feeling. Accepting that truth is easy; using it to create life-changing sermons is not. Experience has shown that some sermons are dynamic and engaging while others are dull and lifeless. That is true, I believe, because some sermons engage the whole person, intellect and feelings, while others are lectures, devoid of passion and feeling. They speak only to the intellect. A sermon that appeals only to the intellect and not to the heart is half a sermon and is doomed to fail.

"One sees clearly only with the heart. Anything essential is invisible to the eye."
—Antoine de Saint-Exupery

If Maya Angelou and Antoine de Saint-Exupery have not convinced you of the importance of touching people's hearts, here is the advice of Pope Francis in an interview published in America magazine, September 30, 2013:

> "...the thing the church needs most today is the ability to heal wounds and to warm the hearts of the faithful..."

A successful sermon which engages the whole person, intellect and feeling, creates an experience which the preacher and listeners share.

If you want to create shared experiences in your preaching, you can learn how. However, you must first learn the crafts of writing and delivering sermons. Good preaching, like good public speaking, is the product of knowledge and skills that can be learned. A good preacher has learned the techniques needed to design sermons, owns the tools and construction materials needed to build them, and has mastered the public-speaking skills needed to deliver them at a professional level. This book will describe those techniques, tools, and skills, and will give you suggestions on how you can make them your own.

In **Part One, "Building the Sermon"**, I will discuss the craft of constructing a sermon, and in **Part Two, "Creating the Unforgettable Sermon"**, I will discuss four catalysts that can transform your sermons so they touch the hearts of your listeners. In **Part Three, "Growing as a Preacher"**, I will offer suggestions on how you can improve your skills, and in **Part Four, "Conducting Retreats and Days of Recollection"**, I will give some recommendations for retreat masters.

Homily or Sermon?

Some churches use the word "homily" to describe preaching during their liturgies while some churches use the word "sermon" to describe their preaching. I will use "homily" only in those instances where it is related to liturgical preaching. Otherwise I will use "sermon."

Scripture and Prayer

I assume we agree that all preaching begins with a reading of scripture and with prayer. Others have developed these subjects better than anything I can add so please include this understanding as you read further. Also, since the sole purpose of this book is to help you with the writing and delivering of your sermons, I will not address the content of your preaching.

Part One

Building the Sermon

When we stand in front of a beautiful painting, we forget that the artist first drew a "cartoon", a sketch, of his first visualization of the picture. As he began to fill in the lines, he became covered with paint and sometimes his own sweat. Painting his work of art was a messy, sometimes dirty, process. So it is with crafting a good sermon. It is usually a messy experience and not pretty at the "cartoon" stage. Still, with hard work, your sermon, like a work of art, can touch people's hearts. Part One is about the messy craft of building the sermon. So roll up your sleeves and let's get to work.

Chapter 1

Some Basic Facts of Life for a Preacher

Preparation

"It usually takes me three weeks to prepare an impromptu speech."
—Mark Twain

No one delivers a good impromptu speech. When a speaker rises to respond to a call for "a few words" and then knocks it out of the park, you can be sure he's given this before or been rolling it around in his mind for hours, maybe days. Good sermons are the products of careful preparation.

Before you begin to put word to paper or computer, you must first admit to yourself that, like an apprentice carpenter, you must first learn the basics of your craft. Both writing and preaching a sermon are crafts. Unlike art which depends upon abilities unique to the artist, a craft can be learned by anyone willing to work at it and learn.

The Craft of Writing a Sermon

"Every man must learn his trade – not pick it up. God requires that he learn it by slow and painful processes. The apprentice-hand in blacksmithing, in medicine, in literature, in everything, is a thing that can't be hidden. It always shows."
—Mark Twain

Twain calls the craft of writing a trade. In that trade (craft), the preacher is like a carpenter. Before building a table, a carpenter must first learn about the different kinds of wood, their characteristics, how to cut and join them, and how to design a strong, beautiful table. Only then can the construction begin. A good carpenter is a good craftsman.

Like the carpenter, the preacher must understand the parts and structure of a sermon, how they fit together, and how to design it. Only then can the preacher write and deliver it. This book will describe the parts and structure of a sermon, the processes of writing and delivering it, and will help you become a better "sermon builder".

> "Writing is [like] making a table. With both you are working with reality, a material just as hard as wood. Both are full of tricks and techniques. Basically very little magic and a lot of hard work are involved."
>
> —Gabriel Garcia Marquez[1]

Chapter 2

The Construction Materials

Health Warning:
This chapter might produce
wide yawns, loud groans and
unintended naps.
Proceed at your own risk.

"I really do not know that anything has ever been more exciting than diagramming sentences."
—Gertrude Stein

Since you probably do not share Stein's enthusiasm for diagramming sentences, I will not inflict it on you, but bear with me. This information is boring but important. You might get yourself a cup of coffee (strong), find a chair (uncomfortable), and get on with it.

Writing Sentences for Immediate Understanding

Why, at this stage in your life, should you read about writing sentences? You have been writing sentences since the third grade. You might even have gained the skill of writing elegant, balanced sentences that run on for four or five lines and can be easily read and understood. The answer to the question is in the words "… be easily *read* and understood."

Because you are writing sentences not to be read but to be heard, some elegant, balanced sentences are not suitable for a sermon. Your goal in writing a sermon is to make it easy for your listeners to hear and understand your message. They need to get it as soon as you say it.

Over the years, I have heard sermons that were full of complex, convoluted, run-on sentences, piled one on top of another. It was such an effort to follow that I frequently gave up trying and drifted away. I suspect many around me did the same.

As a preacher, you write sentences to be heard. Before you wrote for the eye; now you write for the ear. When the readers of your written words don't understand your meaning, they can go back and read it again. When the listeners of your sermons don't understand your meaning, they can't stand up and say, "We didn't get that. Would you repeat it?" Worse yet, you don't know they didn't get it.

Much of your writing education will be useful, but some will not sometimes causing you to write poor, even awful, sermons. The style of writing suitable for reading is different from the style suitable for hearing. So if you want to build understandable sermons, you will have to learn the craft of writing for the ear.

Try this experiment. The next time you are with a group of people and you can just be a member of the group, don't say anything. Listen as they speak with each other. Do they always speak in complete sentences, or do they sometimes use phrases or even one word? Do they speak with dependent clauses or many compound sentences? I think you will hear many simple declarative sentences, phrases or just words. They speak in thoughts. Hear the rhythm and inflections in the voices, the pauses, the passion, the interruptions, the back and forth that no one notices because it is so natural, and no one dozes off. We stay awake and listen when we hear the natural rhythm of conversation.

Writing for the ear calls for a different style of writing, simpler sentence structure that catches the rhythm of conversation. It even breaks the rules you learned over the years. English is a robust, living language. Don't let the grammar police intimidate you.

> "From now on, ending a sentence with a preposition is something up with which I shall not put."
> —Winston Churchill

Ted Sorenson, President John Kennedy's speechwriter, in describing "The Kennedy style of speech-writing", recalled: "...Our chief criterion was always audience comprehension and comfort, and this meant: (1) short speeches, short clauses and short words, wherever possible; (2) a series of points or propositions in numbered or logical sequence where appropriate; and (3) the construction of sentences, phrases and paragraphs in such a manner as to simplify, clarify and emphasize...The test of a text was not how it appeared to the eye, but how it sounded to the ear. His best paragraphs, when read aloud, often had a cadence not unlike blank verse – indeed at times key words would rhyme."[1]

> "The aim of the sculptor is to convince us that he is a sculptor; the aim of the orator is to convince us that he is not an orator."
> —Gilbert Keith Chesterton

Close your eyes and listen to radio or television commercials, not for content but for sentence length and structure. You will hear many simple declarative sentences interspersed with occasional compound sentences and few complex sentences with dependent clauses. The professional writers who craft these series of sentences choose simple, declarative sentences to convey most of their information and use fewer, longer sentences to vary the pattern. They know short sentences are easy to hear and understand.

Professional radio and television writers can teach you how to structure short sentences, but their purpose is not yours. Their purpose is to get quick understanding, not a shared experience. The preacher wants quick understanding also, but in addition wants to create a shared, felt experience that builds community and appeals to the heart leading to conversion. Because preaching a life-changing sermon is more challenging than presenting commercial programs, you must master even more techniques of the crafts of writing and speaking. I will describe them in later chapters.

An exercise I have used in my communications courses demonstrates the difficulty we all have in listening. I wrote a one paragraph description of an incident and made enough copies for everyone in the class. Then I had the students stand in a circle around the room, gave a copy of the paragraph to the first person and asked her to read the paragraph slowly and carefully to the next person. Then that person told the story, without the paper, from memory, to the next person and so on until it reached the last person in the circle. I then passed out the copies to the students, asked them to read it and, after they had finished, asked the last person to tell the story. As the students heard the story, some laughed and others stared in disbelief. Almost always, what they had just heard bore little resemblance to what they just read.

People frequently do not hear what you intend to tell. Therefore, your word choices and sentence structures must be different from what you have used in your writing to be read. To some extent, you must relearn how to write. As a carpenter selects specific pieces of wood to build a table, you choose specific kinds of sentences to build your sermon and reject others.

The basic structure of a sentence is built with a subject (the doer of the action), the verb (the action), and an object (the receiver of the action). All of the added information is placed before, into or after this structure. How you add this information makes some sentences easy to hear and understand and others difficult.

As I describe the different types of sentences, you will see that almost all of them, taken individually, can be heard and understood. The problem is not the individual sentence. It is the cumulative effect of many complex sentences that makes a sermon difficult to follow. For the average listener, the constant effort to pay attention to a sermon full of complex sentences may cause the listener to miss your main idea or worse, leave you entirely. As you read the different types of sentences which I will describe, select the kinds of sentences you will rely on to build your sermons and which you will use less frequently. Your listeners will thank you.

Simple, Declarative Sentences

A simple, declarative sentence (an independent clause) has a subject and a verb, makes a statement and usually ends with a period, sometimes a question mark. In journalism school, they teach "one sentence-one idea", good advice for a preacher too. Use the simple, declarative sentence with one idea as the basic building material of your sermons. Write your sermons the same way you talk – in short, declarative sentences. You are writing for the ear, and your listeners can hear only one idea at a time. You can even violate the rules of grammar and speak in fragments (clauses without verbs) and single words. It is the language and grammar of conversation.

Compound Sentences

A compound sentence is two sentences (independent clauses) joined together by a conjunction (and, but, or). It can create a small problem in writing for the ear. A compound sentence asks your listeners to hear two ideas, a second right after the first. This slightly raises the level of effort needed to understand. If you decide that two ideas go together and you want to keep them together, deliver them with a slight pause at the conjunction to allow your listeners to hear the first idea and to alert them that a second idea is now coming at them.

Example: Peter loved Jesus, (pause) but he denied Him.

Some preachers deliver a different form of the compound sentence. They string together three, four or even more independent clauses, joining them with the conjunction "and." The sentence goes on and on and on. A period after each clause changing them into simple, declarative sentences with micro-second pauses between the sentences will solve the problem.

Complex Sentences

A complex sentence is a sentence (independent clause) coupled with a dependent clause.

A dependent clause has a subject and a verb, but does not make a complete statement by itself. It usually begins with a subordinating conjunction (although, because, when, after…), but needs an independent clause to make sense. Use dependent clauses when you need to show the relationship of two ideas that go together, and two simple, declarative sentences will not allow you to do that.

Example: When we seek God's will, we find life.

When you preach using a complex sentence, your listeners must hear and remember the idea in the dependent clause until you give them the idea in the independent clause. Reading and understanding a dependent clause in a written sentence is easy. Hearing and understanding it as it is spoken in a sermon is different. When a sermon is full of complex and compound sentences, the listeners must work slightly harder to hear the message. They might grow weary of trying to pay attention and drift to more important matters such as what to serve for dinner or what game is on television that afternoon. Be alert to dependent clauses and use them sparingly.

Example: Although sometimes we fail to live up to the Gospel, we know God our Father loves us and will forgive us.

Rewritten: Sometimes we fail to live up to the Gospel, (pause) but we know God our Father loves us. We know He will forgive us.

Compound-Complex Sentences

Compound-Complex sentences are composed of two independent clauses and one or more dependent clauses. Even though the three ideas in this kind of sentence are related, the structure slightly raises the difficulty of hearing.

Example: After the fourth appeal for religion teachers, fifteen people volunteered, and we were able to staff all of the classes.

Rewritten: We made four appeals for religion teachers. Fifteen people volunteered and we were able to staff all of the classes.

Interrupting Relative Clauses

Like dependent clauses, a relative clause has a subject and a verb and does not make a complete statement. It usually begins with a relative pronoun (who, which, whose, that). Relative clauses in the middle of a sentence "interrupt" the flow of the sentence, and are a bit more difficult to follow than a simple, declarative sentence.

Example: Joseph of Arimathea, who was secretly a follower of Jesus, took his body and laid it in his own tomb.

Rewritten: Joseph of Arimathea was a secret follower of Jesus. He took the body of Jesus and laid it in his own tomb.

Sentences with the words "which" or "that" present a similar problem by introducing another idea in a subordinate clause. Put a period in front of those words and begin another sentence.

Example: The teacher pounded on the desk which got the students' attention.

Rewritten: The teacher pounded on the desk. That got the students' attention.

Cumulative Sentences

Cumulative sentences can work well in sermons. A cumulative sentence begins as an independent clause with a subject and verb (a declarative sentence), and then adds more information. Cumulative sentences are easy to hear and understand because the listeners first hear the independent clause with one idea and then hear the other related ideas which amplify that idea. Speaking in Amherst, Maine, on October 26, 1963, John F. Kennedy delivered two cumulative sentences which were in parallel, with repetition and contrasting ideas. I will discuss those techniques in Chapter 9.

"I look forward to a great future for America, a future in which our country will match its military strength with our moral restraint, its wealth with our wisdom, its power with our purpose. I look forward to an America which will not be afraid of grace and beauty, which will protect the beauty of our natural environment, which will preserve the great old American houses and squares and parks of our national past, and which will build handsome and balanced cities for our future."

As you can see from the Kennedy quotation, cumulative sentences draw attention to themselves. They can be used in the Body of a sermon to emphasize an idea that might otherwise be missed because of its location among all the other ideas in the Body.

Your Rhythm

Use the declarative sentence as your workhorse to carry most of your message. At the same time, you want to vary the length of your sentences to avoid a metronome effect. You can create a varied rhythm in your sermon by using short declarative sentences with some cumulative sentences, an occasional complex or compound sentence with a pause at the conjunction or even a single word or phrase. If you read it aloud, you should be able to hear the rhythm. The result will be a conversational sermon that is easy to understand.

Commas

Try not to write sentences with many commas because that means you may have written a dependent clause or interrupted sentence. However, (comma) if you do, (comma) remember that the comma indicates to the reader that here is another idea. Without realizing it, (comma) a reader pauses mentally to get ready for the next idea. When you are speaking your sentences, (comma) your listeners cannot see your commas so you need to pause slightly in your delivery to get them ready for your next idea.

Words

If I ask you to picture an elephant, you see an elephant. However, if I tell you to picture an animal, you might see a dog or a cat. I don't know what you saw because I didn't specify what kind of an animal. Generic or abstract words do not evoke pictures in our minds and therefore have little power to influence. Specific, concrete words do.

> "The difference between the right word and the almost right word is the difference between lightning and the lightning bug."
>
> —Mark Twain

Transitions

Transitions are words or phrases that help readers or listeners follow your moving from one idea to the next.

When you write to be read and you begin a new paragraph with a new idea, your readers can see the new paragraph and understand you are presenting a new idea. When you are preaching and move to a new idea, your listeners cannot see the new paragraph so you need to send them a signal that you are introducing another idea. If you do not send that signal, your listeners might not realize you have moved on to another idea until you have spoken two or more sentences. If you repeat that pattern and make it difficult for them to follow your train of thought, you might lose their attention. At a minimum, it will lessen the effectiveness of your sermon.

In writing to be read or heard, many transitional words or phrases are available. Some of these are: however, in addition, equally important, furthermore, by comparison, and many more. They work well and appear natural in writing to be read, but in preaching, if you use these transitions too much, your sermon can begin to sound like a research paper being read aloud. So how in your preaching do you guide your listeners from one idea to the next without sounding pedantic?

Here is a simple, transitional device that blends well into a conversationally structured sermon and does not draw attention to itself. Include a word or phrase that refers to the idea of your current paragraph in the last sentence of the paragraph. Then repeat that word, phrase, a related word or a synonym, in the first sentence of the next paragraph. This sentence also needs to state the idea in that paragraph. So this sentence then contains a word that refers back to the idea in the previous paragraph and a word that states the idea in this paragraph. You will have created a link between the idea in your current paragraph and the idea in your next paragraph.

Example: You are going to talk about the importance of personal, private prayer and give some suggestions on how to do it. You end your introductory paragraph with this sentence: "One way to learn how to pray is to imitate the lives of holy people who have gone before us." You then begin your next paragraph with: "Jesus frequently left his friends and went off by himself to a quiet place to pray to his father."

The two sentences contain four transitional words and phrases, "holy people" and "Jesus" (related words), and the two words "pray." Your listeners then know where you are going. Of course, they expect you will talk about holy people who knew how to pray and whose lives will show them how to pray.

(Writer's note: In the first sentence, I wrote "Jesus frequently left his friends..." I could have followed my first impulse and written "disciples", but your listeners do not have "disciples"; they have "friends" and must leave their friends to pray. "Friends" makes it easier for them to see what they need to do. It is, as Mark Twain observed, "The difference between the right word and the almost right word...")

The Thing about "Thing"
The word "thing" is a lazy and weak word, lazy because it excuses us from making the effort to search for the exact, specific word

that expresses our idea, and weak because it lacks the strength of the exact, specific word. When you realize you are about to write or say "thing", pause and search for the exact, specific word that expresses what you mean. However, sometimes the specific word might be too strong or draw too much attention to itself for your purpose. The word "thing" allows you to avoid that problem; just make it a conscious decision.

Words and Emotions

Some words recall memories and emotions. If you know your audience well, you can select those words to achieve that effect. Martin Luther King, Jr. knew that for African-Americans the verb "judged" evoked painful memories. It reminded them of when they had been judged guilty by lawless mobs and were lynched. They also were judged in courts without adequate legal representation and finally judged in the silent court of prejudice. So he chose that verb when he said: "I have a dream that my four children will one day live in a nation where they will not be judged by the color of their skin but by the content of their character."

Verbs

The verb is the most important word in a sentence; it gives the sentence its life, its action. It is the one word in the sentence that you want to be "the right word", not "the almost right word."

When you revise your drafts, look for the verb "to be" in all its forms. The verb "to be" just states "being" and links the subject of the sentence with the object. The verb "to be" adds no action to the sentence. It is a weak verb. An example: "The verb is important." can be rewritten as "The verb breathes life into a sentence." When you see you have written the verb "to be", red flag it and, if possible, replace it with an action verb or rewrite the sentence.

> **HINT**: If you are struggling with your rewrite, ask yourself what is the action and who is doing it. Then rewrite with the doer of the action as the subject of the sentence along with the action verb.

Smothered Verbs

A smothered (hidden) verb is a verb turned into a noun. "Jesus took a walk with his disciples." The verb "walked" is smothered in the noun "walk". Unsmothered, it reads: "Jesus walked with his disciples." Better.

As you edit and revise your sentences, ask "What is the action here?" This will lead you to weak and smothered verbs. Then replace them with action verbs.

Buried Subjects

If you notice that you have written a sentence that begins with "There is, There are, There were, It is," you have probably buried the subject of the verb, the doer of the action, in the sentence. Stop. Ask yourself what is the action, the verb, and who is doing the action, the subject of the verb. Then rewrite the sentence beginning with the subject.

Example: There are many Christians who live their lives according to Matthew 25

Rewritten: Many Christians live their lives according to Matthew 25.

Passive Verbs

With two exceptions that I will cover shortly, you should always use the active voice in your preaching. However, I have learned from my writing classes that many well-educated people use passive verbs without realizing it. Sermons with many passive verbs sound stilted, even a bit affected. If you suspect you sometimes slip into the passive without recognizing it, here are some examples to help you spot the passive:

Passive sentence: The blind man was cured by Jesus. In this passive sentence, the doer of the action, "Jesus", is at the end of the sentence in a prepositional phrase and the receiver of the action, "the blind man", is at the beginning of the sentence. Also, the verb, "cured", has a helping verb, "was"

Active sentence: Jesus cured the blind man. Now the doer of the action, "Jesus", is at the beginning of the sentence, and the receiver of the action, "the blind man", is at the end of the sentence. Also, the verb does not have a helping verb.

Notice that when you change the sentence to the active voice, the flow of the sentence moves from the beginning through the sentence to the end. It moves in the same direction as the action that it describes. It sounds natural, not stilted or affected. However, there are two situations in which the passive is useful. The first is when a speaker does not want to say who did the action.

Example in the Active Voice: The head usher stole the Sunday collection. For many reasons, the speaker does not want to name the thief. Change to the passive.

Example in the Passive Voice: The Sunday's collection was stolen. The information is given without naming the doer of the action, the head usher.

The second reason to use the passive is when you want to emphasize the receiver of the action. To do this, move the receiver of the action to the beginning of the sentence, the place of emphasis. First, let's look at a sentence in the active voice:

Active voice: A Roman soldier nailed Jesus to the cross. Because the doer of the action, the Roman soldier, is at the beginning of the sentence, the emphasis is on him. If you do not want to emphasize the soldier, rewrite the sentence in the passive.

Passive voice: Jesus was nailed to the cross. By moving Jesus to the beginning of the sentence and not mentioning the Roman soldier, the emphasis is on Jesus. Even if you include the Roman soldier in a prepositional phrase at the end of the sentence, "by a Roman soldier", the emphasis is still on Jesus.

If you do not have one of these two reasons to use the passive verb, don't. The action in the passive verb sentence flows backwards because the doer of the action, the subject, is at the end of the sentence. It is easier to hear and understand an active verb sentence because the doer of the action is at the beginning. We are able to grasp quickly the flow of the action and the meaning of the sentence. With the active verb, you state your message "head on", the way we talk naturally, and it gives your listeners the impression that you are a straight-talker.

Personal Pronouns

Pronouns "don't get no respect"; they don't have their own identity. The personal pronouns are: I, me, you, she, her, he, him, it, we, us, you, they, them. We hardly notice them but they quietly go about doing their jobs. However, don't underestimate their power to help or hurt you. They can tell your listeners more about you than you intend or even realize.

Let's start with a horrid but true example. A preacher peered down over the pulpit at his listeners, and addressed them as "You people." That pronoun, "you", revealed a great deal about that man, none of it good.

Another lighter example: Every year in the seminary, after our summer vacations, we began the semesters with a retreat. One year a retreat master arrived who referred to himself as "We" and he told us that if we wanted to talk with him, "We will be in our room." (I'm not making this up.) A classmate who had a wonderful sense of humor went to see him. When he returned, he reported, "It's true. They are there."

However, personal pronouns can help you. They can do what their name suggests, make it "personal." "We" implies that we are in this together, a community, and that you are not better than your listeners. You are one of them and you share the same pains, sorrows, failures and joys. The pronoun "I", when you use it well, can serve you in the same way. You can use the "I" pronoun to admit that at times you do not live up to the Gospel message you are preaching.

A reminder: When preaching, be careful using the pronoun "you."

Adjectives and Adverbs

"The adverb is not your friend."

— Stephen King[2]

Adjectives add description to nouns and pronouns. Adverbs add information to verbs, adjectives and other adverbs.

When you use an adverb or adjective, read the sentence without it. If the sentence still gets your message across, the sentence is probably better without it.

Do these added adverbs and adjectives increase the power of this sentence? "We hold these <u>certain</u> truths to be <u>clearly</u> self-evident, that all men are <u>absolutely </u>created equal, that they are endowed by their <u>Almighty</u> Creator with certain <u>fundamental</u>, unalienable Rights, that among these are Life, Liberty and the pursuit of Happiness."

"Less is more."

—Robert Browning

Intensives

Intensives modify another word to make it stronger or more forceful. Some intensives are: very, extremely, really, most, absolutely. Your sermons will be better without them.

> "Substitute "damn" every time you're inclined to write "very"; your editor will delete it and the writing will be just as it should be."
>
> —Mark Twain

Conciseness

> "The secret to being a bore is to tell everything."
>
> —Voltaire

Conciseness does not mean short. It means that every word is necessary and works to move the sentence forward. Consider this poignant short story which Hemingway considered his finest work: "For sale: baby shoes, never worn." It is short but more importantly, it is concise. Every word is necessary and moves the sentence forward until it comes to its heart-breaking ending. The details are precise and efficient with no distracting details.

> "If you would be pungent, be brief; for it is with words as with sunbeams – the more they are condensed, the deeper they burn."
>
> —Robert Southey

Abraham Lincoln's Second Inaugural Address had 701 words. As you read its closing cumulative sentence, can you find any word that does not move it to its conclusion?

"With malice toward none; with charity for all; with firmness in the right, as God gives us to see the right, let us strive on to finish the work we are in; to bind up the nation's wounds; to care for him who shall have borne the battle, and for his widow, and his orphan – to do all which may achieve and cherish a just and lasting peace, among ourselves, and with all nations."

Writing to a friend he had known for some time, Mark Twain said, "I am sorry this is such a long letter, but I did not have the time to write a short one." Writing concise, short sentences does take time and effort. In writing your second drafts, review and judge every word and phrase against the measure "Does it move this sentence forward?" If it doesn't move the sentence forward, take it out or replace it with a word that does. Your more concise sentences might shorten your sermons considerably but better a tight ten minute sermon than a fifteen minute long and flabby one. If you fear your listeners will not hear and remember what you will say because your sentence is so concise, repeat your idea again with different words a second time.

Reread the last paragraph ignoring the underlined words and see how much better the sentences move forward without them.

"Be sincere; be brief; be seated."
—Franklin Delano Roosevelt

If you want your sermon to be a shared experience, you are more likely to reach your listeners' hearts with concise, efficient sentences.

Paragraphs

Even in writing for the ear, you need to organize your thoughts in paragraphs. Each paragraph introduces a new idea. The topic sentence in a paragraph states the new idea and every sentence in the paragraph must relate to and support that idea.

In Summary

This chapter has been about the construction materials, some strong and clear, some weak and confusing, from which you can choose to build your sermons. If you build with strong and clear sentence structure, your listeners will hear and understand your message. Just as a carpenter must pay attention to the small details to build a strong table, you must pay attention to these small details to build strong, successful sermons.

PRACTICE

The next time you attend a meeting with speakers, if you can, ignore the content and listen to the sentence structure. Do the speakers use short, declarative, active voice sentences, or do they use dependent clauses, independent clauses joined by many conjunctions (and..and..and...), many adjectives, adverbs and weak verbs? This experience will sensitize you to the importance of sentence structure in public speaking. Then write your next sermon using sentences to be heard.

End of Health Warning:
Resume full speed.

Chapter 3

The Three "Essentials" for a Successful Sermon

"Essential" Number One: Purpose

"You've got to be very careful if you don't know where you are going because you might not get there."
—Yogi Berra

A *superior sermon will have one primary purpose* and possibly a secondary purpose. Yogi got it right. You need to know where you are going with your sermon. If you don't, your listeners will sense it and will tune-out. The usual purposes of sermons are either to persuade, move to action or instruct. The meanings of "persuade" and "move to action" are clear. The meaning of "instruct" is not. For a preacher, imparting knowledge is not enough. That is a lecture. This question then arises: What does the preacher want them to do with the knowledge – act on it, reaffirm their faith in that knowledge, or simple to rejoice in it as good news in their lives?

Secondary Purpose

A secondary purpose must be related to and support your primary purpose. If it does not, your listeners will sense you have headed off in another direction and must struggle to follow you. For example, if your primary purpose is to persuade your listeners of the importance of praying every day and your secondary purpose is to show how to pray daily, your secondary purpose clearly relates to and supports your primary purpose. But to change the example slightly, if you have the same primary purpose, the importance of personal prayer every day, but your secondary purpose is to instruct them in the history of prayer in the Church, it doesn't really support your primary purpose. It is related but distantly.

> **PRACTICE**
>
> *Identify your primary purpose and your secondary if you have one. Write it in a simple, declarative sentence. After you have decided upon you purpose, you are then ready to identify your one main idea.*

"Essential" Number Two: One Main Idea

A good sermon has one main idea. All of the other ideas and facts in it must support that one main idea. That idea creates a theme which runs through the sermon and unifies it. When your audience hears the conclusion, they agree and accept it because everything they have heard leads up to it. If asked, your listeners should be able to answer immediately what your sermon is all about, your main idea. Your purpose and your one main idea are so closely related that discovering one will usually lead you to the other. Sometimes you find your main idea first, and that leads you to your purpose.

The Preacher's Temptation – Those Other Great Ideas

"It was hard to have a conversation with anyone. There were so many people talking."

—Yogi Berra

Yogi got it right again. When there's too much chatter going on, it's hard to hear the conversation. Any idea or fact that does not support the main idea is a distraction.

During the cold war, US bombers carried bits of metal foil to drop if radar guided missiles were fired at them. The thousands of metal foil bits, "chaff", would confuse the missile's radar and it would miss its target. In your sermon, bits of unrelated ideas and facts, "chaff", confuse your listeners as they try to lock onto your one main idea. If those bits continue, your listeners become tired of the effort and drift away.

So what do you do with those other great, too-important-not-to-discuss ideas? Professional writers are guided by a saying: "Kill your darlings." If a fact or idea does not support the main idea, you must take it out. You might love the idea and congratulate yourself on how well you have crafted this precious jewel, but it is a temptation. Take it out. Be ruthless. If it's that good, it might be the main idea for another sermon, another day.

> **PRACTICE**
>
> *Pull out a recent sermon and review it for your one, main idea. Write it in a simple, declarative sentence. Then review your sermon for any ideas that do not support the main idea. Resolve to be ruthless in deleting them in the future.*

"Essential" Number Three: Call to Action

"The test of a good preacher is that his congregation goes away saying not "What a lovely sermon," but "I will do something about it."

—St. Francis de Sales

When you identify your purpose ("Essential" Number One), remember that a sermon is not a lecture; it cannot just instruct or persuade. The fundamental purpose of all sermons is to change people's lives, to move them to desire a deeper relationship with God. Some movement, either an internal change of heart or a follow-up action, must happen. So at the end of your sermon, suggest a specific action they can perform to make what they have heard real in their lives. And it should not be a "lettuce" action: "Let us always remember the example of the saints as we go about our daily lives." A "lettuce" action is useless. It does not ask your listeners to take any meaningful action. If you find you are ending your sermon with a "lettuce" action, it might mean you did not identify your purpose clearly in your own mind. The "Call to Action" flows from your purpose.

Your listeners need a specific action they can take to apply what they have learned from your sermon. It can be something simple like a reminder to read the Bible every day and pray over it, or to search for Him at a local "Food for the Poor" center. You can reinforce your Call to Action by asking the choir director to select a related song at the dismissal.

If you are preaching a retreat, you might not want to include a "Call to Action" on each occasion you speak. However, you need to consider what it will be and build toward it.

> **PRACTICE**
> *Review your Call to Action to determine if it flows naturally from your main idea and purpose. Does it challenge your listeners?*

More Writing Tips – Sharpen the Focus

The sharper the focus of your main idea, the more likely you are to develop it so it can be understood. If you decide to talk about

Salvation History from Abraham to Jesus, you have a broad area to cover and a difficult job covering it in twelve minutes. If you decide to talk about what Jesus said about salvation, you have a more manageable job. To make sure you have sharpened the focus of your main idea, write it in one, simple sentence, no dependent clauses or conjunctions.

Emphasis

All sermons have three parts, the Introduction, the Body, and the Conclusion. The Introduction, usually one paragraph, tells what will be developed in the Body. The Body, made up of many paragraphs, contains the ideas that support and develop the main idea. The Conclusion brings the sermon to a close.

All writing, including a sermon, has two places of emphasis, the beginning (the Introduction), and the end (the Conclusion). They are the places of relative emphasis because they are the first and last ideas your listeners hear. Everything in the middle – the "in-between" ideas, (the Body paragraphs), have slightly less emphasis. The beginning and end are also places of opportunity.

The Introduction gives you the opportunity to make two important points: first, to introduce your main idea, and second, to place your "hook." I will cover the "hook" next. The Conclusion of your sermon gives you the opportunity to reinforce your main idea and to give your "Call to Action."

The next time you open your morning newspaper, read one or two of the more accomplished sports or opinion columnists. Notice how they use the first paragraph to introduce the main idea along with a hook. After that, go to the last paragraph to see if they have in some way repeated or reinforced that idea. They probably will not include a "Call to Action" because that is not their purpose. However, if their purpose is to persuade you to agree with them, they might use the last paragraph to state one final idea to persuade you. Professional writers know how to take full advantage of those two paragraphs. Imitate them by writing your main idea in your introduction in a simple, declarative sentence. Then reinforce it in your conclusion with some form of restatement and your "Call to Action." I suggest you write your first and last paragraphs in full and deliver them word for word as you have written them so you can be certain your listeners have heard and understood your main idea and your "Call to Action."

Some preachers waste the opportunity in the Introduction by using it to repeat the scripture readings, sometimes in excruciating detail. If you have inflicted this agony on your listeners, admit your guilt, and resolve never to commit it again – please.

The "Hook"

Skilled public speakers grab their audience's attention right away by writing a hook into their Introductions. A good hook is based on the needs of the listeners or the needs of others with whom they can empathize. Abraham Maslow told us that our needs are arranged in an ascending hierarchy, from the most basic to the highest level of self-fulfillment, and that we must first satisfy our lower needs before moving higher. At the bottom are our physiological needs for food, water, air, shelter, warmth, sex and sleep. After we have satisfied them by finding a job and a place to live, we want to keep them. So we move up to the next level, our safety needs – security, protection, order and stability. Once we have a secure job and a safe place to live, we can move up to enjoy family and friends, our social needs. We then aspire for achievement, status and reputation, our esteem needs. When we have satisfied these four levels of needs, we can then move up to the highest level, self-actualization, and seek personal growth and fulfillment. Before you begin to analyze your listeners' needs, consider first where you live on Maslow's hierarchy. The fact that you are reading this book says that you probably have a college degree with post-graduate studies, do not have to worry about your next meal, or where you will sleep tonight, have a secure job with a modest income, and have a circle of friends who share your beliefs and values, welcome you into their company and hold you in esteem. A further indicator of where you are on Maslow's hierarchy is your desire to preach the Gospel, self-actualization at the highest level. Now you are ready to consider your listeners' needs. While many of them might appear to enjoy full lives with all five levels of their needs met, many live with threats to their needs. Some worry about losing their jobs, some their homes to foreclosure, and some their marriages through divorce. Others suffer from loneliness or depression. In order to write a hook that works, a preacher needs to be sensitive to the listeners' needs. A hook that recognizes these needs will invite their attention and encourage them to listen.

Sometimes you might discover the hook as you write your Introduction with its main idea, or it might come to you as you develop the Body of your sermon. You can then go back and insert the hook into your Introduction.

A hook must be honest, not a gimmick. To be honest, a hook must relate to the purpose and main idea, the more obvious the better. If it is a gimmick, the listeners will sense it is not honest and might be less open to your message. An example of a gimmick is a humorous story for a quick laugh, but a funny story introducing the main idea is not. This true, humorous story could be used as just a gimmick or as an honest hook to introduce the main idea:

When the actor Thomas Mitchell visited his friend, W. C. Fields, a lifelong agnostic, on his deathbed, he found

Fields reading the Bible. "What are you doing reading a Bible?" asked the astonished Mitchell. Fields answered, "I'm looking for loopholes."

At a moment of crisis in his country, President Franklin Roosevelt wrote this opening paragraph in his speech to the nation: "Yesterday, December 7, 1941, a date which will live in infamy, the United States of America was suddenly and deliberately attacked by naval and air forces of the Empire of Japan." The President appealed not only to the self interests of Americans for security from foreign attacks, but also to the American sense of fair play and described the attack as "... a day which will live in infamy." Their anger aroused, his countrymen were ready to listen to what their leader had to say. His hook worked.

Here is a hook from our master storyteller: "..., A man was going down from Jerusalem to Jericho, and he fell among robbers, who stripped him and beat him, and departed, leaving him half dead." (Luke 10:30) His audience heard the account of a violent crime, theft, escape of the guilty and a man dying. Who would not want to know what happened next? They are now ready to hear the lesson Jesus is going to teach them.

PRACTICE
If your Introduction does not have a hook, write one.

Listening to Your Audience
When I was newly ordained and young, I did not know the needs of the people in the parish, and my sermons reflected my lack of understanding. They were sermons based on the textbooks I had read in the seminary. I talked "at" my listeners. Now I am older and have learned some of those needs, sometimes painfully. But

you can learn those needs without the pain. You can move beyond the textbooks and even Maslow's hierarchy by talking and listening to the people to whom you preach.

Years ago I worked with a man who moon-lighted by selling special-interest articles to local newspapers. He told me that he was amazed how people would share intimate details of their lives with him just because he was a reporter. You are more than a reporter. If in your conversations with friends and even strangers, you ask what they need from your sermons, I suspect that like my friend, you will be amazed how people will share with you. Listen and keep the 3" by 5" cards handy.

PRACTICE

Spend some time working to get to know the deeper needs of your listeners, either by talking with them over a cup of coffee, or sharing insights with others who preach to the same audience.

Humor

"A nun, a rabbi, and a priest walk into a bar. The bartender looks up and says, "What is this? A joke?""

Some believe that preachers should not attempt humor in their sermons. It can be risky, and I agree that humor that does not support the main idea is a gimmick and a distraction. Also, jokes that are poorly built and delivered deserve the groans they are met with. However, all humor is based on our not taking ourselves too seriously, an essential ingredient in Christian humility.

If you are not convinced, you might read *Between Heaven and Mirth*,[1] by James Martin, S.J.. Martin writes that "...joy, humor, and laughter do not lie outside the believing life, but are at the heart of it. They *are* the heart of that life." He tells us that many of Jesus' parables were humorous and quotes Daniel Harrington, a New Testament scholar, about them: "Humor is very culture-bound...I suspect that the early readers found these stories hilarious, whereas we in a very different social setting miss the point entirely." An example Martin uses is the parable of the rich man about to go on a journey who gives money to his servants to invest, five talents to one, two to another and one to the last. Martin then tells us that "...for the listeners of the day, there would have been a clear element of the absurd in the story, for a "talent" was the equivalent of a worker's daily wages for *fifteen* years. The idea of a wealthy man blithely handing over to one of his servants an extraordinary sum – seventy-five years of wages! – would have evoked a sense of the ridiculous in his hearers. Jesus was not above using a little comic exaggeration to make a point."

Martin tells a number of humorous stories and jokes, but my favorite is one that could be used in a sermon during Christian Unity Week:

"There is a story about people from different religious denominations who are traveling on a bus to an ecumenical conference for Christian Unity Week. While singing songs together, they become so distracted that they run off the road and hit a telephone pole, die, and go to heaven.

The crowd meets St. Peter, who welcomes all of them. "Okay," he says. "First the Episcopalians. Welcome to heaven. Since you've all led good Christian lives and enriched us so much liturgically, go into Room Five, but on the way make sure not to look inside Room One." The Episcopalians walk happily over to Room Five.

Then he says to the Baptists, "Welcome Baptists. Thanks for all the great preaching and witnessing you've done during your lives. Why don't you take Room Two, but make sure not to peek into Room One."

Then he turns to another group and says, "Methodists, nice to see you! Thanks for leading such good Christian lives and for all those great hymns. Why don't you all go into Room Three? But make sure not to go into Room One."

Finally, one of the Methodists says to St. Peter "Can I ask you something? What's in Room One?"

St. Peter says, "Oh, that's where the Catholics are. They think they're the only ones up here."

Shakespeare also understood the importance of humor. A rule of playwriting is that the more serious the action of the play, the greater is the need for humor. Shakespeare inserted humor, some of it earthy, in many of his serious plays. We see this instinctive need for relief in humor at funerals when friends and family tell funny stories about the person they loved and lost. Not all of us are good at this but if a funny line or joke occurs to you about your serious subject and is not a gimmick but builds your main idea, don't be afraid of it. Your listeners will enjoy it and be grateful. Here's one you can use when talking about how difficult it is for some people to believe:

An atheist and Jesus went fishing together. An oar fell overboard and drifted away from the boat. Jesus got out of the boat, walked to the oar, picked it up and carried it back to the boat. Later someone asked the atheist how the day went fishing with Jesus. "It was a good day but can you believe it," he said, "that guy can't even swim."

Quotations

A well-structured quotation can express your main idea so well you listeners will think, "Yes, that's true." When it is from a famous person we don't expect it from, the surprise is an unexpected pleasure. The opening quotation in this book from George Burns about sermons is that kind of a quotation. Humorous quotations on a serious subject can "help the medicine go down."

The Internet is a gold mine for quotations. A few minutes search will yield more than you can use. Just enter you main idea and if you want humorous quotations, add "humorous." The quotations throughout this book and the thirty-one quotations in the Appendices might give you a sense of the possibilities.

> **PRACTICE**
>
> *Begin a file of quotations and humorous stories that you might use.*

Chapter 4

More Writing Tips

What the "Wizard of Menlo Park" Knew

When Thomas Edison was struggling to solve a problem, he took naps. Edison anticipated the work of modern neuroscientists who have studied the influence of sleep on creativity and memory. They have discovered that sleep helps both the creative process and memory building.

While neuroscientists debate among themselves exactly how the brain does this, most of them agree that sleep significantly improves the creative process and memory building. As Matthew Walker, Assistant Professor of Psychology, Harvard Medical School, said: "Practice makes perfect but only if you sleep on it."[1]

Try to begin your creative process early enough so you can get a night's sleep after you have completed your first attempts; then begin again the next day. In practicing your sermon, don't practice on the day you will speak. Practice a day or two before your preaching and allow your brain to work on it while you sleep. It will reinforce your memory of what you plan to say.

JULIA SLEPT AND ABRAHAM WEPT

In 1862, Julia Howe, at the urging of a friend, began to think about writing new words to a popular but crude Civil War song. She later wrote: "...I went to bed and slept as usual, but awoke the next morning in the gray of the early dawn, and to my astonishment found that the wished-for lines were arranging themselves in my brain.

I lay quite still until the last verse had completed itself in my thoughts, then hastily arose, saying to myself, "I shall lose this if I don't write it down immediately. I searched for an old sheet of paper and an old stub of a pen…and began to scrawl the lines almost without looking…" Abraham Lincoln reportedly wept when he heard her transformation of "John Brown's Body" into "The Battle Hymn of the Republic."

PRACTICE

Keep an "old sheet of paper and an old stub of a pen" next to your bed while you sleep to capture your new inspirations before they vanish.

The Problem of Not Enough Time

"Until we can manage time, we can manage nothing else."

—Peter Drucker

Planning is the key to managing and leveraging your time. A good place to begin is to consider the findings of an Italian economist, Vilfredo Pareto. In 1906, Pareto observed that 80% of the land in Italy was controlled by 20% of the population. His observations became known as the Pareto Principle (the 80/20 rule), also applicable to other situations in life. Contemporary data supports Pareto's original findings. In the United States in 2007, 85% of "privately held wealth" was owned by 20% of the population which left 15% of the wealth for the remaining 80% of the population, (G. William Domhoff, University of California at Santa Cruz).[2] If we look at "financial wealth" (total wealth minus the value of one's home), 20% of the population owned 93% while 80% owned 7%.

Applying Pareto's research in the 1940's, Joseph Juran, an expert in quality control in business, reversed the numbers and referred to this 20% to 80% ratio as the "vital few and the trivial (useful) many." He said that only a few, 20% of the actions we perform, are vital and produce important, valuable results. The remaining 80% produce only useful results. Juran used the Pareto Principle in his consulting with many Japanese companies which contributed to improvements in their quality control and dominance in world markets.

Steven Pearlstein[3] refers to the Pareto Principle as "...the remarkably robust observation that organizations often achieve 80 percent of what they want to accomplish with 20 percent of their people and resources."

In the United States, twenty percent of Americans who drink account for 80 percent of the alcohol consumed and the same 80-20 ratio is seen in users of illegal drugs.[4]

To help you begin your time management planning to leverage your time, here are some strategies from the time management experts that you might find helpful:

- First, identify your vital, 20% tasks that will produce your 80% important, valuable results. If you have difficulty identifying them, consider meeting with some colleagues who have the same ministry to work on them together. You might interview a few "customers" to find out what they see as your "vital few."

- Second, identify your 80% tasks that will produce 20% useful but trivial results

- Schedule the first appointment of your day with yourself, about 10 to 15 minutes, to plan and manage the day.

- Schedule your vital, 20% tasks according to the expected results and determine if you can do all of them or do you need to ask for help. This is where you will leverage your time.

- If possible, delegate all or most of your trivial, 80% tasks. Consider what will happen if you just don't do some of them. Sometimes you need to say "no."

"The graveyards are full of indispensable men."

—Charles de Gaulle

- Carry and use a portable planner, either paper or electronic. Create a coding system to identify your vital few and trivial many. You might use A for your vital few, B for your important tasks which are not vital but you must do that day, and C for your trivial many. Then number each task within each category 1, 2, 3, etc. to decide which you will do first. You might not work on all of your A's every day, but you need to keep them before you every day.

- Since early morning is most people's high-energy time, work on your A's and B's then. Because your C's are usually easier, "busy" work, they will tempt you to waste your time with them. Resist the temptation.

- Handle and complete one task at a time. Multi-tasking is inefficient and confusing.

- For those big problem tasks that you wonder where to start, brainstorm it into pieces and jot down your thoughts. Come back to them the next day.

- End every day by taking ten minutes to think about the next day and jot down your thoughts. It will give you a start on your next morning's scheduling time, and you can sleep on it overnight.

"The key is not to prioritize your schedule, but to schedule your priorities."

—Stephen Covey

- I assume we agree that preparation and practice of a sermon is a vital, 20% task that produces 80% important, valuable results. It is always an A.

To Write or Not to Write in Full

The question of whether it is necessary to write your sermon in full reminds me of a sign I saw in a dentist's office:

PATIENT: "Doctor, do I have to floss all my teeth?"
DOCTOR: "No. Only those you want to keep."

Sign in my office:

YOU: "Do I have to write my sermon in full?"
ME: "No. Only those parts you want to be good."

When I prepared a sermon, I jotted down my key ideas, arranged them in order with some lead off words or phrases, practiced in my room, and went with it. I realize now the results reflected my preparation or rather my lack of it. Later, when I became a trainer, I taught a wide range of courses using written instructor manuals. From my years of speaking in front of classes, I learned that preparation is everything. If I didn't know what I wanted to accomplish with a class and what I was going to say, I was in trouble.

Similarly, every preacher is faced with the same problem of preparation and its related question of how much of a presentation to write – full text or key words. From my research, public speaking mentors today recommend that you think of your talk as existing in two different documents. The first is the text that you write. The second is the text you use to deliver it. You can create your delivery text quickly if you write your first text on your computer. Then use the copy and paste function to transfer words or phrases into your delivery document. Bolding the text and increasing the font size and line spacing will make it easier to scan as you preach. If you prefer to go with 3" x 5" or 5" x 7" cards, a felt-tipped black pen will do the job.

The experts' thinking is that in order to preserve spontaneity and authenticity in your delivery, it is better to work from key words or phrases to remind you of what you are going to say and what comes next. Reading from a fully written text will possibly deaden your delivery. Some even recommend not using any notes at all. They advocate practicing until you feel you have complete control of your content and then speak from memory. Obviously there is no one right answer so you need to find your comfort level.

The same experts also recommend writing your "speech" in full. Their reasoning is that if you decide you want to use some of the techniques I will describe in chapters 6 and 7, stories and rhetorical figures, you will need to write them in full. Stories require multiple rewrites before they work, and rhetorical figures also need careful thought and structuring. You want to be certain that your Introduction contains your main idea and your hook, and that your Conclusion quickly summarizes your sermon and announces the "Call to Action." Also, if you want to mimic the rhythm of conversation with short sentences, pauses, phrases and single words, can you do that "on the fly?"

When you write your sermons in full, you are in good company. Public speakers who have written their speeches in full include Cicero, Abraham Lincoln, Winston Churchill, John Kennedy, Ronald Regan and Martin Luther King.

A Compromise

If because of your experience you believe you can mimic the rhythms and sentence variations of conversation without writing everything in full, I offer you a compromise. Write in full the two places of emphasis, the Introduction and the Conclusion, and the more demanding techniques, stories and rhetorical figures.

However, if you sometimes tend to use weak verbs, the passive voice, unnecessary adverbs, adjectives, or too many words (not concise), you might want to impose on yourself the discipline of writing in full. Tough medicine but your listeners will appreciate it.

Developing Your Ideas So Your Listeners Will Hear

Writing sermons to be heard requires not only constructing sentences that can be easily understood, but also developing the main idea in a manner that fits with your listeners' primary thinking tendencies. They will then be more receptive to your message and more inclined to accept it.

> "The moment you realize that *it's not what you say that counts in the end, but what the audience hears,* you will be on the road toward becoming a great, charismatic speaker."
>
> —Nick Morgan[5]

With the invention of functional magnetic resonance imaging, neuroscientists have been able to map and discover the functioning of different parts of the brain. They have discovered, not surprisingly, that female and male brains, while mostly similar, are different in several important characteristics.

The scientists warn that their descriptions are generalized tendencies, and that some men have some female brain tendencies, and some women have some male brain tendencies. The differences do not indicate superiority, just different functioning.

"I hate women because they always know where things are."

—James Thurber

They have discovered that female brains are hard-wired for empathy, getting in touch with their feelings and those of others, verbal language, details, and emotional memory. Simon Baron-Cohen says that "the male brain is predominately hard-wired for understanding and building systems."[6] He defines systemizing as "… the drive to analyze, explore, and construct a system. The systemizer intuitively figures out how things work, or extracts the underlying rules that govern the behavior of a system. This is done in order to understand and predict the system, or to invent a new one."

The result of these differences is that sitting before a preacher are people with difference thinking tendencies. Some have strong relational tendencies with some systemic, and some people with strong systemic tendencies with some relational. The challenge facing the preacher then is how to develop the main idea to appeal to both brain tendencies.

If you feel inclined to dismiss this research as the impractical theories of ivory-tower academics, spend a few minutes on-line with companies that specialize in marketing. Enter "difference between marketing to men and women." These people are not interested in saving souls. They are the ultimate pragmatists. Their focus is on the bottom-line, making money, and they demand measurable results. I think reading what they have to say will convince you that you need to remember these different thinking tendencies when planning your sermons.

A review of idea development techniques will give you the options available to you. Idea development usually falls into one or more categories, but the primary ones are Deduction and Induction. The other seven can be used within the first two.

1. **Deduction:** (A process of reasoning from general premises to a conclusion.) In this approach, your main idea is derived from your premise, and is stated in the introduction along with the hook. The body paragraphs then examine and develop the idea. Because this approach is similar to the structure of a research paper which analyzes and develops a thesis, I believe it is a systemic exploration of the idea and appeals to the intellect, the head. "Since God created us in His image, all human life is sacred."

2. **Induction:** (A process reaching a conclusion from particular instances.) As in deduction, the preacher knows the purpose, main idea and hook. The main idea and hook can be one or several sentences in the Introduction which present a statement to be verified or a problem to be solved. The examples or stories in the Body enable the listeners to begin to answer the question or resolve the problem on their own. Stories help them verify the truth of the events from their own memories and accept them.

The preacher can then use these particular instances in the Body to lead the listeners to the resolution of the problem stated in the last paragraph, the Conclusion. That paragraph also contains the "Call to Action." I believe this approach lends itself to a relational development which appeals to the heart. For example, by describing in stories the actions of some members of the church in service to the poor, the listeners can see what lives lived according to Matthew 25 look like and inspire them to imitate their lives by responding to the "Call to Action."

The purposes and main ideas of some sermons require deductive development. For example, if a preacher's purpose is to help his listeners understand a complex reality of Christian life, the main idea, and persuade them to accept it in all of its complexity, a rational, systemic approach is appropriate. Then in order to appeal to the listeners' need for a relational application that touches their hearts, the preacher could tell a story that illustrates how it works in real life. A preacher using the inductive approach could insert a short, systemic explanation to satisfy the male brain tendencies. Some development techniques can help the preacher "hedge" the deductive or inductive approaches so the sermon appeals to both brain tendencies. These techniques are:

3. **Classification**: "The books of the Bible are divided into…"
4. **Authority**: "The Bible tells us that…"
5. **Cause and Effect**: "The invention of the pill led to the sexual revolution which in turn…"
6. **Narrative**: This gives a chronological description of a series of events.

7. **Illustration**: After making a statement, you give an example: "People in our church are trying to live by Matthew 25. For example, some volunteer once a week at "Food for the Poor." Some visit the prison once a month."

8. **Analogy**: This compares two ideas which are similar in some aspects, one of which is difficult to understand or accept. "Devoting time to prayer with Jesus is like spending time in the company of a good friend. You don't always have to talk; just be silent, listen, and enjoy the moment."

9. **Compare and Contrast**: This could be a description of the lives of two people, a person whose focus in life is money, and a person whose focus is in service to others.

A free online video sponsored by Boston College gives a helpful description of the deductive and inductive approaches. You can find it at: www.bc.edu/ preaching. It will take you to "Touchstones for Preaching." Then under "Basic Touchstones", select 4, "Shaping the Homily." Clicking on that will take you to the video.

Developing Your Ideas with a Homily Preparation Group

The 1982 Bishops' document, "Fulfilled in Your Hearing", recommends working with a homily preparation group. You can find directions for downloading the document in the Appendices.

The document suggests a seven step process (pages 37 and 38) to guide the group in their discussion. It begins with reading the scriptures, and then allows the members to share their insights into the readings. Someone who studied the scriptures before the meeting then shares additional reflections. Next the members are asked what good news they heard in the scriptures, and what challenges and consequences they see in their lives in the readings. Finally, they end the meeting with prayer.

I suggest you recruit someone from outside of the group to facilitate the meeting. That will allow you to be a member of the group and direct all of your attention to hearing what the members are saying. Both are full time jobs and few people can do both well. You will be better able to spot an insight that you think will help you and you can ask the person to tell you more.

If a member mentions a true incident that interests you and you think it could become a story you might use in a homily, ask if you both can meet after the meeting to write it. Remember to ask for permission to use it.

If you decide to work with a sermon preparation group, some research by Assistant Professor Anita Woolley, Tepper School of Business, Carnegie Mellon University, might help you in recruiting and working with your group.[7]

Professor Woolley set out to study why some groups seem to produce better results than others. Working with small groups, she first tested the intelligence levels of the members. She then tasked the groups with problem solving exercises. She found that groups, like individuals, have a "collective intelligence", and that the groups' "collective intelligence" were higher than the average of their members' intelligence levels. However, the "collective intelligence" of groups varied from group to group. The question then arose: Why do some groups have a higher "collective intelligence" and also produce better results? By observation, testing and measurement, she was able to identify three factors that caused these variations.

The first and most important cause was "social sensitivity." "Social sensitivity" is the ability to read other people's feelings, mostly through their facial expressions and body language. The testing revealed that among the members of the groups, the women scored higher in "social sensitivity" than the men.

The second cause was how equally the members took turns in speaking. Groups in which some members took more than equal time did not perform as well as groups in which members shared the speaking time equally.

The third cause was the proportion of women in the groups. The groups' "collective intelligence" and the quality of their production were higher in proportion to the number of women in the group. A higher number of women in the groups raised their "collective intelligence" and the quality of their production.

You can profit from Professor Woolley's research in forming your homily preparation group by selecting people with high "social sensitivity", who do not dominate a discussion, and a high proportion of women.

Chapter 5

The Process of Writing a Sermon

"Writing a column is easy. You just sit in front of a typewriter until small beads of blood appear on your forehead."

—Red Smith[1]

Unlike *Red Smith*, you don't have to bleed to write a good sermon. Professional writers know that writing is a process. Some who have been writing for many years may have forgotten that at one time they had to learn the process, step-by-step. If you learn and follow the process, you will write more easily, and your final product will be better. The process will transform you into a writer. Some writing teachers have four steps, others more. I have customized the process for you into five steps.

The process as you see it here is linear, one step after another. In reality, it is a messy, back and forth movement in which you discover what you are creating as you go along. Follow the process, but feel free to use it as a guide, not a strait-jacket. Use whatever works for you.

You will notice that the five step process takes place over several days. Because preaching is one of your "vital few", you need to schedule step 1 at least 3 or 4 days before you will deliver your sermon.

If you work with a homily preparation group, their insights will give you the ideas you need for steps 1 and 2. Otherwise you will have to complete steps 1 and 2 yourself.

The Five Step Process for Writing a Sermon
1. Prepare
2. Brainstorm
3. Organize
4. Write
5. Revise

If possible, schedule a night's sleep either between steps 2 and 3, or between 3 and 4.

Step 1: Prepare
In your preparation you answer four questions:
a. What is my purpose?
b. What is my "one, main idea"?
c. What is my "hook"?
d. What is my "Call to Action"?

When you know your primary purpose, you can identify your one, main idea. Frequently you recognize both at the same time. To make sure you have one, main idea, try writing it in a simple, active voice sentence. As stated earlier, a sermon can have a secondary purpose. Make sure now that the secondary purpose supports your primary purpose. Your "Call to Action" should follow naturally from your purpose.

PRACTICE
After you have considered these questions, write your answers in four declarative sentences:

Step 2. Brainstorm
Anne Lamott in her book, <u>Bird by bird: some instructions on writing and life</u>,[2] recounted a moment in her family's life. Her

older brother sat at their kitchen table, unable to begin writing a report on birds that was due the next day. He sat there, she said, "...immobilized by the hugeness of the task ahead." Their father, a professional writer, sat down beside her brother and said, "Bird by bird, buddy, just take it bird by bird."

Brainstorming helps you generate the content of your sermon "bird by bird." If you have never trying brainstorming in writing your sermons, you might want to experiment with it. You can brainstorm by yourself or with a sermon preparation group; more on that shortly. If you choose to write by yourself, write your ideas in words or phrases, if necessary short sentences, as they come to you. Do not eliminate anything. Just get it down. If this is a subject you know well, this process may take five to ten minutes. If you have to do some research, it will take longer. If possible, give yourself enough time so you can "sleep on it" with a pad and pen beside your bed. When you begin the process again, you are likely to have new ideas, possibly even a different purpose and main idea. When you can't think of anything more to add, the brainstorming is finished.

Step 3. Organize

Now is the time to organize your brainstormed list of ideas into a sequence that the ideas themselves suggest. Like the sculptor searching for the statue in the block of marble, you search for the innate order of the ideas.

You have three different techniques available to you for organizing your ideas:

1. Organize them in your head (difficult if not impossible). Juggling ten to twenty ideas in your head, then identifying them as major or supporting ideas and finally putting them in proper sequence would tax even an Einstein's brain.

2. If you have brainstormed on your computer and all your ideas are on one screen, you can organize them using "cut and paste."

3. If your ideas have scrolled onto another screen, you will probably find it easier to print them and work from hard copy.

Here's how to organize using hardcopy:

- Identify your main ideas as best you can at this stage of the process.

- Write them in sequence in their "innate" order. They will be the topic sentences of your paragraphs.

- Connect the supporting ideas to their major ideas with lines or numbers.

- Rewrite your organized ideas into an outline indenting the supporting ideas under their major ideas. You will find it easier at this point to spot and delete facts or ideas which do not support your main ideas. You will also notice gaps where additional information is needed and you can add it now.

Brainstorming is a creative, back and forth process. You may discover even in the organizing phase that you are developing another main idea and purpose, not what you had originally thought. Go with it. Keep the brainstorming process open for that creative growth. Keep your list of ideas with you through the day, and add ideas as they come to you, "bird by bird". Once your brain understands what you are trying to do, the ideas will come. Be ready to capture them at the moment or they will fly away, not to return.

Before you dismiss brainstorming as too time consuming, remember that you must generate and organize your ideas, no matter how you go about it. In brainstorming, you first concentrate your attention on generating your ideas. By deliberately postponing the work of how you will express these ideas in writing, you keep the creative process open for more, varied ideas. Do not shut down this process too soon. Your best sermons will rise out of this raw material. The creative, generative process completed, you are then ready to begin the hard work of structuring your ideas into sentences and paragraphs.

Some people in my writing classes object that they don't have time to do all the pre-writing work in steps 1, 2 and 3. My response is: If you want to produce good writing, you will have to do this work sooner or later. It's easier and faster to do it up front. If you postpone it, you will have to figure it out as you write, an inefficient way to go about it. It will take more time, not less.

Step 4. Write

Clear writing is the result of clear thinking, and the purpose of this five step process is to help you think clearly. In Step 2, you brainstormed the ideas that will be the content of your sermon and in Step 3, you organized them into an "innate", logical order. At this point, you have made your first stab at establishing those "logical relationships." You may change them again and again.

You are now ready to write your words and phrases into sentences, your first draft. When you have difficulty in getting started on a sentence, stop and ask yourself: "What am I trying to say?" Frequently that will get you to a simple, declarative sentence. Yet even after all of this work, many experience some degree of writer's block. I believe it arises from a form of perfectionism. We want our first drafts to be perfect.

Your First Drafts

Many years ago I attended the Breadloaf Writers' Conference in Middlebury, Vermont. One of the faculty authors told about his problem with first drafts. As he typed his words on the typewriter, he knew what he wrote was garbage. After tearing page after page out of his typewriter, he stopped to reflect about what he was doing. He realized that he was holding himself to a writing standard he couldn't meet in his first draft. After that, he gave himself permission to write garbage and began to write.

All first drafts are garbage. As you write your first drafts, give yourself permission to write garbage. It makes life a lot easier and you will get on with it.

> "The waste basket is the writer's best friend."
> —Isaac Bashevis Singer

Step 5. Revise

> "I'm not a very good writer, but I'm an excellent rewriter."
> —James Michener

After all your hard work, you have more to do. You need to revise your drafts to produce your final working copy. The experts tell us that an audience listening to a speaker has an attention span of about six to eight minutes. You continue to revise your draft to use those eight minutes to achieve your purpose.

> "A designer knows he has achieved perfection not when there is nothing left to add, but when there is nothing left to take away."
> —Antoine de Saint-Exupery

Now is the time to rework for conciseness. You must kill the adjectives and adverbs, the passive and the "to be" verbs and the ideas and facts that do not support your main idea. Replace weak verbs with action verbs. Review your sentences so they have one idea expressed in conversational words. Rework the pattern of your sentences so that most of them are declarative or cumulative sentences with few compound or complex sentences. Insert single words or phrases when appropriate. Read them aloud to hear if they mimic the rhythm of conversation.

Just as multi-tasking in your work is inefficient and confusing, trying to work simultaneously on all five steps is inefficient and confusing. As you have seen, the process separates writing into its component parts. By doing this, it allows the writer to focus on each step before moving on to the next. The result is usually clearer thinking and better writing.

Freewriting
If you decide that you do not like the brainstorming technique for generating your ideas, freewriting is an alternative approach. First, make sure you know your purpose and main idea. Then you just write in sentences and paragraphs as your ideas come to you. After you have completed your first draft, revise until you are satisfied you have your final version. I still believe that you are not working as efficiently and effectively in freewriting as you would with the brainstorming approach. In freewriting, you are simultaneously brainstorming, organizing and writing, but if you are comfortable with it and freewriting works for you, stay with it.

The Hybrid Approach
Another approach is to use a hybrid version of the five-step process and freewriting. In this, you first identify your purpose and main idea and then brainstorm your ideas. Next go to

freewriting, crossing off your brainstormed ideas as you include them in your freewriting. You get the benefits of brainstorming and still work in freewriting to produce your first draft.

The Appendices contain a check list, "The Process of Writing a Sermon." It will help you remember the sequence of the techniques in this book as you create and revise your sermons.

Your Final Revision

The structure of your completed sermon will now look something like this:

INTRODUCTION:

- Introduces your one, main idea which establishes the theme that runs through your sermon and unifies it.

- Presents your "hook" based on the needs or interests of your listeners.

- If possible, tells a story. If you do not tell a story in the Introduction, you can tell it in the Body. I will discuss stories in Chapter 6.

BODY:

- Presents the facts and ideas that develop your theme. The first sentence, the topic sentence in a paragraph, introduces the one idea of that paragraph and is a place of emphasis. Even if you do not write a sermon in full, these sentences are important enough to write and revise. They become an outline of your sermon. If you write a sermon in full, someone should be able to read just the topic sentences and see how you developed the theme.

CONCLUSION:
- Repeats and concludes your main idea.
- Announces your "Call to Action".

The Seminary Department of the National Catholic Educational Association conducted a research study into what Catholics want in preaching. The number one quality which 83% of the respondents identified was: "The message is clear and well-organized." Number two was: "It holds my attention." You can request a copy of the report by contacting the Seminary Department of the National Catholic Educational Association at: www.seminary@ncea.org.

If you want to give your listeners what they have said they want, I suggest you follow the process in this chapter. Clear, well-organized writing is the result of critical thinking and this process helps you to think critically. Follow the process.

Writer and Editor

Publishers hire professional writers and editors. The writers do the creative part, getting the ideas on paper. The editors do the critical, evaluative part. Both are essential to producing a quality piece of writing.

Like the publishers' professional writers, you must still sit down and write your sermon. It is your creative process. That process gives you the forward motion to generate ideas and the words and sentences to express them. It also blinds you to the gaps and errors in your writing. When you have finished your revised draft, you must then become your own editor, something the publishers organize themselves to avoid. They know how difficult it is to edit our own writing.

The only way for you to solve this conflict is to separate your editing from your writing. Sleeping on it for just one night will let you read it with fresh eyes and see the gaps and mistakes. Try to get started early in the week to give your draft cooling off time.

PRACTICE

Use the process to prepare your next sermon.

We have completed the process of building and writing a sermon and are now ready to study the four catalysts that will transform and lift your sermon to a shared experience. But before we proceed, I share with you some advice from the past.

First, Do No Harm

The ancient counsel to physicians, "First, do no harm", also applies to preachers. An unfortunate word or phrase, spoken on impulse, or an idea developed without reflection, can cut like a surgeon's scalpel and inflict a hurt that will last a lifetime.

Some people might tell you they found your comment hurtful, but most will quietly walk away and you will never know, a tragedy for both of you. Like the physician, the preacher's job is to heal and strengthen, an awesome responsibility. On those occasions when you decide to talk about our shared failures to live our lives according to the Gospel, you might reflect on this observation by William Osler, M.D.[3]:

"The good physician treats the disease. The great physician treats the patient who has the disease."

Part Two

Creating the Unforgettable Sermon

"Whatever touches the heart will
always be engraved on the mind."
—Voltaire

Maya Angelou's insight "…people will never forget how you made them feel." and Voltaire's observation are wise advice for those who preach. In Part Two, I will discuss four catalysts that can transform your sermons so they touch the hearts of your listeners. If you include these four catalysts in your sermons, you will create experiences which your listeners will not forget. The four catalysts are: Stories, Rhetorical Figures, Your Passion, and Your Delivery.

Chapter 6

Catalyst Number 1: Stories

"Tell me a fact and I'll learn.
Tell me a truth and I'll believe.
Tell me a story and I'll remember it forever."
—Indian proverb

Aspiring young writers learn early in Creative Writing 101 about the power of "show" stories. In a "show" story, a writer does not "tell" the reader what the writer's conclusion is about a person or a situation. She "shows" the reader the details surrounding the person and allows the reader to reach the conclusion.

Here are two versions of the same event. First the "tell":

It was the girl's first little league softball game and she was nervous. Her mother could see her nervousness and tried to calm her on the way to the game, but it didn't seem to help. Nevertheless, she played the whole game and seemed to have enjoyed the experience. It had meant a lot to her.

The "show" version:

Jeannie was happy about her seventh birthday because it meant she now could play little league softball like her Mom and Aunt Mary. She went to all the practices and finally the first game came. As they drove to the game, Jeannie was quiet and her hands were clenched. She was nervous. She played second base, made one error with a dropped fly, but in the bottom of the last inning, she got a double. When the next batter hit the ball over the shortstop's head, Jeannie took off for home. All her teammates were waiting for her as she scored the winning run. Then she ran to her Mom with a big smile, and with her hand up for a "high five", said; "Mom, that was fun. Thanks for teaching me to play."

"Until a fact passes through your imagination, it is a lie."
—Stella Adler[1]

Stella Adler's advice for her student actors is also helpful for the preacher. Abstract concepts like love, hate or service are not lies, but they do not move us. They do not have flesh and blood; they are not real. You must pass them through your imagination to make them true, to give them flesh and blood, to make them real. "Show" stories do that.

Why Stories Work
The research findings of neuro-scientists help us understand how "show" stories give abstract ideas flesh and blood. They tell us that many experiences we have lived are stored in our brains, waiting for us to recall them. Michael O'Shea, a neuroscientist, describes what he calls "Episodic memories":

"Episodic memory corresponds to our memories of past events or episodes...episodic memories are personal, highly selective, idiosyncratic, and possibly false, but they may also be richly complex and movie-like in character. They constitute the stories we tell ourselves about our past, they are the things we would write about in our autobiography. Episodic memories can be recalled deliberately or are triggered by evocative sensory stimulus."[2]

O'Shea also tells us that "...emotional association is a powerful facilitator of long-term memory formation."[3] Daniel

Levitin, also a neuroscientist, emphasizes the importance of emotion in forming long-term memory: "Memory strength is also a function of how much we care about the experience. Neurochemical tags associated with memories mark them for importance, and we tend to code as important things that carry with them a lot of emotion, either positive or negative." [4]

Some neuroscientists and psychologists refer to this experience as "narrative transport." In a 2004 study, researchers had volunteers "read a short story about a gay man attending his college fraternity's reunion. Those who had friends or family members who were homosexual reported higher transportation, and they also perceived the story events, settings and characters to be more realistic. Transportation was also deeper for participants with past experiences in fraternities or sororities."[5]

These long-term, "episodic" memories have implications for what you decide to say in your sermons because your listeners have these stored memories and emotions waiting to be recalled. Stories can transport them back to the joyful events in their past, but also to the unwanted painful memories that can haunt them for years. Stories can not only allow them relive the happiness of their joyful moments, but also can exorcise the demons of the past, soothe the pain and heal the wounds.

"If stories come to you, care for them. And learn to give them away where they are needed. Sometimes a person needs a story more than food to stay alive. That is why we put these stories in each other's memory."

—Barry Lopez [6]

Examples of Stories That Work

Harriet Beecher Stowe passed the facts of slavery through her imagination to write a fictional "show" story, "Uncle Tom's

Cabin." Abraham Lincoln recognized the power of her story when, upon meeting her, he said: "So you're the little lady who started this great war."

Jesus told "show" stories all the time and he chose his details carefully to stimulate his listeners' long-term memories. Many of them had seen shepherds guarding their sheep, farmers sowing seed, and poor people for whom every penny counted. So when Jesus told his stories about the shepherd with the lost sheep, the seed falling on barren ground, and the poor woman who lost a penny, the brains of his listeners instantly recalled those memories and understood and responded to the messages of his stories.

Today when preachers talk about the parables in their Sunday sermons, they frequently feel compelled to explain the history and circumstances of the time. They realize that their listeners, unlike Jesus' listeners, do not have these experiences stored in their long-term memories.

Some of his parables, however, are close enough to our experiences that we instantly connect with them; "… But while he was yet at a distance, his father saw him and had compassion, and ran and embraced him and kissed him." (Luke15:20) Most of us have memories from our earliest days of a father or mother who loved, hugged and kissed us. They are likely our oldest and most cherished memories. In addition to the message about how God loves us, for many Christians this is their favorite parable because it evokes memories of the times in their lives when they felt most deeply loved.

THE FATHER

I visited a young man who was dying of Aids. As I was leaving, I asked him if there was anything else I could do for him. He said "yes"; he would like to see his father whom he had not seen in some time. I knew the man because he was at daily mass and communion. When I told the father that his son was dying and wanted to see him, he replied, "I have no son."

—Father Dick Martin[7]

A "show" story appeals to our heart as well as our head. A real life example of love in action can move us to tears, is easy to understand, remember, and possibly imitate. The abstract concept leaves us cold. In the story of the prodigal son, we feel the presence of the father's love and it warms us. In the story of the father with the dying son, we feel the absence of love and it chills us.

The last four words of "The Father" remind me of the advice the Russian ballet impresario, Serge Diaghilev, gave the young writer, Jean Cocteau: "Astonish me!" Unlike Cocteau, you do not write to entertain, but you do want to tell stories that will astonish your listeners with a moment of revelation into a truth of life that relates to the Gospel. The story, "The Father", is a good example. It astonishes us as it shows the father's lack of self-knowledge and hypocrisy while at the same time, it reminds those of us open to the full meaning of the story of our own self-deceptions and petty hypocrisies. Some stories astonish dramatically and forcefully, others quietly and softly. In the Appendices, you will find eight true stories. When you read them, you might pause after each one and consider if it astonished you and in what manner. Also, notice how the author used the last sentence, the second place of emphasis, to heighten that effect.

The Power of Stories
Many years ago, I took two semesters in short-story writing. The instructor read our stories aloud and then we discussed them.

After he read several of mine, I was astounded at the interpretations and meanings the other students saw in my stories, meanings that I had not intended or even conceived of. From that I learned that even though people listen to the same story, each person hears a different story. Each person brings past memories and emotions to the experience of hearing your story and finds different meanings in it. Those individual meanings go to the essence of why you tell stories and are what give your stories their power. So after you have told your story, do not explain it too much, if at all. A well-written "show" story speaks for itself. Give your listeners room to move around inside your stories, to hear again the details that bring back the memories and emotions that touch their hearts.

Some of the memoires will be joyful, some will stir regret and others will recall painful experiences. Knowing this, you can then move on in developing your sermon to celebrate again the joy, forgive the regrets, or heal the pain.

A well written "show" story develops your main idea, raises the emotional level of a sermon, and creates a shared experience. If you have never considered yourself a storyteller, relax. I will show you how to write a story, but first read this poem by the American poet, Marie Howe.[8] Notice the verbs, adjectives, and nouns (the details) she chooses to "show" Jesus to us through the people he loved. After you have finished, reflect on what your saw through the details as you read it.

THE STAR MARKET[9]

The people Jesus loved were shopping at The Star Market yesterday.
An old lead-colored man standing next to me at the checkout breathed so heavily I had to step back a few steps.

Even after his bags were packed he still stood, breathing hard and
hawking into his hand. The feeble, the lame, I could hardly look at them:
shuffling through the aisles, they smelled of decay, as if The Star Market

had declared a day off for the able-bodied, and I had wandered in
with the rest of them: sour milk, bad meat:
looking for cereal and spring water.

Jesus must have been a saint, I said to myself, looking for my lost car
in the parking lot later, stumbling among the people who would have
been lowered into rooms by ropes, who would have crept

out of caves or crawled from the corners of public baths on their hands
and knees begging for mercy.

If I touch only the hem of his garment, one woman thought, I will be healed.
Could I bear the look on his face when he wheels around?

You might never write poems like Marie Howe, but you can
write "show" stories.

How to write "show" stories

Some people say they can't tell a joke. The reason is because they
don't realize that a joke has to be set up and built. Once a joke
has been properly "set up" for the punch line, the teller just has to
deliver it as "built" and enjoy the laughs. A "show" story also has
to be "built."

Here's how to build a "show" story. After you have found a
true life story that can reach the hearts of your listeners, you first
need persons with whom your listeners can identify. They don't
have to like them; just be able to recognize them. Second,
something significant happens, the sooner the better. Third, the
persons come up against a problem. Fourth, the story comes to a
conclusion, sometimes inspiring or shocking, sometimes happy or

sad. If the story truly "shows", the teaching is clear right away; the preacher does not have to explain it and is free to continue to develop the main idea.

As you develop your story, give the concrete details which allow your listeners to see the events of the story as they unfold. Robert De Niro, the actor, said, "It's all in the details."[10] The details take your listeners back to the auto-associated details of similar experiences stored in their memories. There they can test the details of your story against their remembered details and decide if the story is true.

If Jesus wanted to tell us His Father loves us and said: "My Father always loves you and is ready to forgive you", would it have moved you? Probably not. Instead, he passed the "facts" through his imagination. Then in the story, the father "...ran and embraced him and kissed him." This was an old man who ran, not walked, to his son, put his arms around him, didn't shake his hand, and in an intimate gesture, kissed him. The image of the father running down the road to his son, throwing his arms around him and kissing him, gives us a moving picture that shows us how much the father loved his son. With these details and our memories of similar experiences, we don't have to be "told" the father loved his son. We see and feel it right away.

A "show" story in a sermon must be concise and short. Here are a few hints to help you:

- A story must support your purpose and main idea. If it doesn't, it is a distraction. It might be appropriate for another sermon with a different purpose.

- Keep the number of persons in the story to two or three. More become confusing. If the story involves more than two or three, give the "show" details about them and use "tell" to describe the rest. For example, if the story is about a confrontational moment at a family Thanksgiving dinner, "show" the details about the people involved with the dialogue and "tell" about the other people and the result: "Everyone looked down at their napkins and the room went silent."

- Stick to the important characteristics of the people; don't expand their personalities beyond what is necessary for the story: "I knew the man because he was at daily mass and communion."

- Establish the situation right at the beginning: "I visited a young man who was dying of Aids."

- The story should cover a short time span. You don't have time for more.

- Avoid abstract words. Use specific details (imagery) so you create a short moving picture which your listeners can see and hear.

- Dialogue gives the listeners a sense of being there, watching and listening to the action as it is happening, and they sense it is true; "I have no son."

- A rule about playwriting says: "If you hang a pistol over the mantel in the first act, fire it by the third act." This also applies to your "show" story. Most of your stories will revolve around a fact that you express in a word or phrase. Write that word as early in your story as is suitable; "hang the pistol." Then, if possible, use the same word at the end of your story, "fire the pistol", so you make it easy for your listeners to hear the same fact in the same word, or a synonym; "...a young man who was dying of Aids."... "his son was dying"... "I have no son."

- "Astonish" your listeners with your last sentence.

- Because "show" stories must be concise, you need to rewrite it until you are sure every detail moves the story forward to its conclusion and you have not included unnecessary details. Read again Father Martin's story, "The Father", and notice how every detail is necessary. Less is more.

Lawrence Olivier, speaking of acting, said, "Everything you do should be autobiographical."[11] That is also true of storytelling. Your best stories will be about events you witnessed and participated in. Your listeners know your story is true because you were a part of it and are a witness to its truth.

"...good art deals with the micro to explain the macro...there's something in the very small minutia of life that tells us something about the big, big picture that we see every day all over the place,...the more specific and creative and revelatory you are in the micro, the more powerful the macro will be."
—Philip Seymour Hoffman[12]

Here is a story that describes a micro event in the life of the author. The readers can then apply the revelation in the micro event to the macro "...big, big picture" in their lives.

THE HUNGRY BOY

I visited Haiti as part of our participation in a "Food For The Poor" pilgrimage. At the feeding center in Port-Au-Prince, I met a little boy who had picked up a bucket of rice and beans. Other children were digging into their buckets, hungrily eating the food with their hands. I asked the boy why he wasn't eating and he said "because today is not my day to eat."

—Jim McDaniel

"Description is revelation."

—Gerard Manley Hopkins

I prefer true stories for the reasons I have already discussed, but sometimes a fictional story supports your purpose and main idea so well that you might want to use it. Here is a fictional story that you could use when preaching about the importance of drawing apart to a quiet place to meet God in silence.

THE RABBI'S CHILD

A rabbi had a child who used to stray off into the forest. At first his father let him stray. But when it got to be a regular routine, the father grew concerned. What was his child doing there? Besides, the forest was dangerous. One day he asked the child, "Why do you go into the forest each day?" The child said, "I go to find God." The father responded, "That's a wonderful thing to do, my child. And I'm pleased you search for God. But, my child, you should realize that God is the same everywhere." The child answered, "I know that, Father; but I am not the same everywhere."

—Rabbi David Wolpe[13]

Consider adding short stories to your recreational reading. While short stories are longer than your stories and their purpose, entertainment, is different, their structures and techniques are frequently similar. Because the author writes for the "eye" instead of for the "ear" as you do, the sentence structure will be more complex and unsuitable for your purposes. However, much will be useful. As you read a short story, look for the hook and how the author establishes the situation in the beginning. Notice the main idea or theme that gives unity to the story. See the "show" details and figure out why the author uses the "tell" in some places in the story. Hear the dialogue and sense how it lets you listen in to the action as it takes place. If you have the opportunity, consider taking one or two semesters in short story writing. Learn how to pass facts through your imagination.

To show you that stories are all around you, here is an incident from my life. I was shopping at Safeway, picked up three items and, as I put them on the check-out conveyor belt, I noticed a man standing behind me. When I glanced at him, he smiled and said "Hello." I replied "Hello" and then pointed to one of my items and said "This is on sale. It's a good buy." He said "My wife can't eat that. She had a stroke eight years ago. I take care of her." I said "You're a lucky man to have your wife. My wife died eight years ago." He said "Sorry. I know I'm a lucky man. I love my wife." I said "You're a good husband to take care of your wife like you do." He said "Oh, I love my wife. I love my wife." I replied "I loved my wife too." A voice to my right said "Please swipe your card sir." I paid and then turned to the man. He smiled, waved and said, "Take care." I waved back, "take care." The stories are all around you. Talk with people and listen. They want to tell you their stories.

> "There is no greater agony than bearing an untold story inside of you."
>
> —Maya Angelou

Your own life experiences, past and present, are your gold mine of "micro" raw materials for your true stories. The trick is in spotting them. Frequently they are so ordinary, we don't see them.

PRACTICE

Think of some event in your life that would make a good "show" story. Write it and put it aside for two or three days. After it has cooled off, revise it. File it for when you can use it and resolve to include one story in every one of your recollections or sermons.

Writing stories is a skill. The more you write, the easier it becomes. Stay with it. Continue to look for events in your life that can become your "show" stories. Write them while the details are fresh in your mind and add it to your file.

HINT: Carry 3"x 5" index cards with you to capture the details. I have found that if I don't write them when they happen, they are frequently gone forever.

———

BONUS: The index cards will remind you to live in the moment. You will see grace in the ordinary.

Chapter 7

Catalyst Number 2: Rhetorical Figures

Rhetoric is the study of structuring language, sometimes to instruct, but more frequently to persuade and move an audience. Its development goes back to the ancient Greeks and Romans. From those times and through the Middle Ages, the study of rhetoric was considered an essential part of a complete education, especially for a person preparing to speak in public. The study of the subject of rhetoric is beyond the scope of this book. However, I will discuss some of the writing techniques of rhetoric which are known as rhetorical figures. Rhetorical figures (figures) are techniques for structuring sentences and paragraphs to increase their power to persuade, uplift, or affect the audience in some manner. They are especially useful to the preacher who can use them to emphasize the main idea or an important supporting idea, and then persuade the listeners to accept and act upon it.

Rhetorical figures in their various forms run into the hundreds so this short treatment can only introduce you to some of them. However, with study you can begin to use them immediately. I will give you a brief description of some with their Greek names and then a few examples.

Isocolon (ai-so-*co*-lon): To create this figure, usually referred to as parallelism, the speaker uses successive sentences, clauses, or phrases with the same structure, length, and rhythm.

> "...Render therefore to Caesar the things that are
> Caesar's, and to God the things that are God's."
> —Matthew 22:21

"Let every nation know, whether it wishes us well or ill, that we shall pay any price, bear any burden, meet any hardship, support any friend, oppose any foe, in order to assure the survival and the success of liberty."

—John F. Kennedy
Inaugural Address

"The moral test of government is how that government treats those who are in the dawn of life, the children; those who are in the twilight of life, the elderly; and those who are in the shadows of life – the sick, the needy and the handicapped."

—Hubert Humphrey

"The louder he talked of his honor, the faster we counted our spoons."

—Ralph Waldo Emerson

"My mother thanks you, my father thanks you, my sister thanks you and I thank you."

—George M. Cohan

"Of all the gin joints, in all the towns, in all the world, she walks into mine."

—Humphrey Bogart (Rick)
Casablanca

Anaphora (a-*na*-pho-ra): With this figure, the speaker repeats the same words at the beginning of sentences.

"...Blessed are the poor in spirit, for theirs is the kingdom of heaven.

Blessed are they who mourn, for they will be comforted. Blessed are the meek, for they will inherit the land...."
—Matthew 5: 3-5

"We have also come to this hallowed spot to remind America of the fierce urgency of Now. This is no time to engage in the luxury of cooling off or take the tranquilizing drug of gradualism. Now is the time to make real the promises of democracy. Now is the time to rise from the dark and desolate valley of segregation to the sunlit path of racial justice. Now is the time to lift our nation from the quicksands of racial injustice to the solid rock of brotherhood. Now is the time to make justice a reality for all of God's children."[1]
—Dr. Martin Luther King (August 28, 1963)
The "I Have a Dream" Speech

"At times, history and fate meet at a single time in a single place to shape a turning point in man's unending search for freedom. So it was at Lexington and Concord. So it was a century ago at Appomattox. So it was last week in Selma, Alabama."
—Lyndon Johnson (March 15, 1965)
To a joint session of Congress

Epistrophe (e-*pis*-tro-phee): This figure repeats a word or phrase at the end of a series of sentences or phrases, sometimes in an order of increasing intensity.

"In the beginning was the Word, and the Word was with God, and the Word was God."
— John, 1:1

"...that this nation shall have a new birth of freedom, and that government of the people, by the people, for the people, shall not perish from the earth."

—Abraham Lincoln
Gettysburg Address

"They have no vision, and when there is no vision the people perish."

—Franklin D. Roosevelt
First inaugural address
speaking about the bankers of the time

"If you want to see the girl next door, go next door."

—Joan Crawford,
responding to a question why she
always dressed-up when she went out.

Symploce (*sim*-plo-see): This figure combines anaphora and epistrophe. Words are repeated at the beginning of sentences and other words are repeated at the ends.

"When I was a child, I spoke like a child, I thought like a child, I reasoned like a child; when I became a man, I gave up childish ways."

—1 Corinthians 13:11

"My brother need not be idealized, or enlarged in death beyond what he was in life, to be remembered simply as a good and decent man, who saw wrong and tried to right it, saw suffering, and tried to heal it, saw war and tried to stop it."

—Senator Edward Kennedy

"When there is talk of hatred, let us stand up and talk against it. When there is talk of violence, let us stand up and talk against it."

—Willliam Jefferson Clinton

Chiasmus (kai-*as*-mus): In this figure, the words are reversed.

When the persistent Canaanite woman pleaded with Jesus to heal her daughter, Jesus answered, "It is not fair to take the children's bread and throw it to the dogs." The woman replied: "Yes, Lord, yet even the dogs eat the crumbs that fall from their masters' table."

—Matthew. 15:26-27

"Ask not what your country can do for you, ask what you can do for your country."[2]

—John F. Kennedy
Inaugural Address

"Your manuscript is both good and original; but the part that is good is not original, and the part that is original is not good."

—Samuel Johnson,
responding to an aspiring novelist who
asked to have his manuscript reviewed.

Anadiplosis (a-na-di-*plo*-sis): This figure repeats the last word or clause to begin the next. It often leads to climax.

"More than that, we rejoice in our sufferings, knowing that suffering produces endurance, and endurance produces character, and character produces hope,…."
—Romans 5:3-5

Polypton (po-*lip*-tou-ton): Words derived from the same root are repeated.

"Divine Master, grant that I may not so much seek to be consoled as to console; To be understood as to understand; To be loved as to love; For it is in giving that we receive; It is in pardoning that we are pardoned; And it is in dying that we are born to eternal life."
—Prayer of St. Francis of Assisi

"Let me assert my firm belief that the only thing we have to fear is fear itself."
—Franklin Delano Roosevelt
First Inaugural Address, 1933

Polysyndeton (po-ly-*sin*-de-tahn): With this figure, the speaker repeats conjunctions along with a series of ideas. Through this piling-on of related ideas, the writer develops and emphasizes the main idea of the sentence or paragraph.

"Both parties deprecated war, but one of them would make war rather than let the nation survive, and the other would accept war rather than let it perish, and the war came."
—Abraham Lincoln
Second Inaugural Address

"If you are ready to leave father and mother, and brother and sister, and wife and child and friends, and never see them again – if you have paid your debts, and made your will, and settled all your affairs, and are a free man – then you are ready for a walk."

—Thoreau

Asyndeton: In this figure, the writer omits conjunctions when they might be expected.

"But, in a larger sense, we cannot dedicate, we cannot consecrate, we cannot hallow this ground."

—Abraham Lincoln
Gettysburg Address

Antithesis (an-*tih*-theh-sis): occurs when the speaker juxtaposes two contrasting ideas, usually in parallel structure.

"Think not that I have come to abolish the law and the prophets; I have come not to abolish them but to fulfil them."

—Matthew 5: 17

"You have heard that it was said, 'You shall love your neighbor and hate your enemy.' But I say to you, Love your enemies and pray for those who persecute you,…"

—Matthew 5: 43-44

"The world will little note, nor long remember, what we say here, but it can never forget what they did here."

—Abraham Lincoln
Gettysburg Address

"I have a dream that my four little children will one day live in a nation where they will not be judged by the color of their skin but by the content of their character."
—Martin Luther King

Hypophore (hy-*pop*-ho-ra): occurs when the speaker asks a question and answers it.

"Are they Hebrews? So am I. Are they Israelites? So am I. Are they descendants of Abraham? So am I. Are they servants of Christ? I am a better one – I am talking like a madman – with far greater labors, far more imprisonments, with countless beatings, and often near death."
—2 Corinthians 11:22-23

"No foresight can anticipate, nor any document of reasonable length contain express provisions for all possible questions. Shall fugitives from labor be surrendered by national or State authority? The Constitution does not expressly say. May Congress prohibit slavery in the Territories? The Constitution does not expressly say. Must Congress protect slavery in the Territories? The Constitution does not expressly say.
—Abraham Lincoln
First Inaugural Address

Prolepsis (pro-*lep*-sis): occurs when the speaker anticipates an objection and answers it.

Some say that Christianity is heading for extinction in developed countries, but I say they forget what the Holy Spirit has done in difficult times in the past.

Enallage (en-*al*-uh-jee): occurs when the speaker changes the expected sentence structure, frequently in an ungrammatical form.

"We was robbed!"

—Joe Jacobs

Fight manager after his fighter lost on decision

"Your father he is."

—Yoda

Star Wars Episode VI: Return of the Jedi

"I don't get no respect."

—Rodney Dangerfield

Using Rhetorical Figures in Your Sermons

The first step in writing a rhetorical figure in your sermon is to go back to your purpose and main idea. Since a figure emphasizes the idea it is expressing and trys to persuade the listener to accept it and perhaps act upon it, you want the figure to support your main idea or one of its supporting ideas.

A good example of an orator knowing his purpose and main idea occurred during the dark days at the beginning of World War II. Winston Churchill, speaking before the House of Commons, sought to rally the British people, strengthen their resolve, and convince them of final victory. (Pop quiz: Did you notice the rhetorical figure in the sentence you just read? Answer is after the Churchill quote below.)

In his speech, Churchill chose anaphora and repeated the pronoun and verb "We shall". In the relentless rhythm of that repetition, we can almost hear the beat of the drummer on the battlefield encouraging the soldiers to fight bravely. He constructed this figure to emphasize his purpose and main idea and wrote a speech that would be remembered through the ages:

> "We shall go on to the end, we shall fight in France, we shall fight on the seas and oceans, we shall fight with growing confidence and growing strength in the air, we shall defend our Island, whatever the cost may be, we shall fight on the beaches, we shall fight on the landing grounds, we shall fight in the fields and in the streets, we shall fight in the hills; we shall never surrender..."

(Answer to the Pop quiz: You can see parallelism (Isocolon) in the three phrases beginning with the infinite verbs "...to rally...(to) strengthen...(to) convince..." It is hardly memorable prose but better than "He wanted to encourage the British people to fight.")

In order to select the appropriate figure, you should be familiar with the figures most frequently used. Reading examples of rhetorical figures is the best way to learn them. You might borrow from your library or even buy one of the many books on rhetoric. Once you have a working familiarity with many figures, you can reflect on the nature of the idea, scan the types of figures, and decide which of them will work for you. The process is part analysis and part creative intuition.

Parallelism is one of the easier figures to learn and works well in preaching. To create a parallel sentence, first identify the idea you want to emphasize. Then find one or two ideas which closely express the same thought. Your computer's thesaurus can help. Some writers believe you need at least three ideas to make it work. Then write the ideas using the same structure. Use all nouns, adjectives with nouns or phrases with the same form of their verbs with similar objectives. You want your listeners to hear the same pattern and rhythm in all three ideas.

In the Appendices under "Web Sites", you will find a site titled "Parallelism in Abraham Lincoln's Gettysburg Address." In it you will discover that Lincoln wrote his entire speech in parallel. He drafted it on the train from Washington to Gettysburg and completed it in his room the night before he delivered it. It is testimony to Lincoln's masterful command of language and rhetorical figures.

If you enter "parallelism" in your computer's search engine, you will find many sites with examples and exercises. Whatever time you spend there will pay you back in more compelling sermons.

Earlier I wrote of the importance of using active voice, declarative sentences in your sermons to assure that your listeners hear and understand your message. Using rhetorical figures does not contradict that advice. When you occasionally use sentences with rhetorical figures, your listeners will sense the change in your rhythm, will notice your emphasis, and will pay closer attention.

In the Appendices you will find thirty-one quotations. When you read them, notice how many are rhetorical figures. After reading the quotations, you might go back and study them to see how the authors structured the sentences to create rhetorical figures.

> **PRACTICE**
> *Look for suitable opportunities to use figures, especially to emphasize your main idea.*

Chapter 8

Catalyst Number 3: Your Passion

"Expecting the world to treat you fairly because you are good is like expecting the bull not to charge because you are a vegetarian."

—Dennis Wholey [1]

Even though you are faithful to your Baptismal commitments, you live a modest life and pray daily, all this is hidden from most people in the pews. They know you only from what they hear in your voice and see in your gestures. As with the bull and the vegetarian, unfair as it may be, if your voice is flat and your body language is wooden, they will judge you to be lukewarm to what you are saying. But if they hear and see passion, they will judge that you believe what you are saying.

Many preachers by education, temperament and culture feel uncomfortable, even insincere, when speaking in an emotional or animated manner that is not them. You must speak in your own voice. John Wayne learned this the hard way when he played Genghis Khan in "The Conqueror", regarded as one of the worst films ever produced. Wayne realized he had been miscast in the role, and was embarrassed that he did not perform well. He later remarked that the lesson he learned was "not to make an ass of yourself trying to play parts you're not suited for." Like Wayne, you cannot and should not try to be someone you are not, but if you believe and feel passionately about what you are saying, you must let your listeners see and hear and feel your passion.

TEACHER TO CLASS: "Why do we keep silent in church?"
JOHNNY: "I know. I know."
TEACHER: "Why Johnny?"
JOHNNY: "Because we don't want to wake up the people who are sleeping."

The passion you bring to your sermons is like the music in movies. Play again in your mind the music in the movie "The Magnificent Seven." If you can't recall it, search on the Internet for "The Magnificent Seven – Elmer Bernstein". Without the music, Yul Brynner and his gang are just a bunch of guys on horses. Add that lyrical, driving music, and they become avenging knights riding to rescue the hard-working, good farmers from the thieving, evil bandits. Passion in your sermon is the music that transports you and your listeners to a place higher than what your words describe, a shared experience. A sermon without passion is like a movie without music. If you allow your passion to animate your preaching, your preaching will become music that inspires your listeners and changes their lives.

An Example – A Speech with Passion:
Sojourner Truth (Isabella Baumfree), born a slave in 1797, suffered beatings, abuse and terrible hardships until she seized her freedom by walking away. After being "overwhelmed with the greatness of the Divine presence", she joined the Methodist Church and later became a traveling preacher. In 1854, at the Ohio Woman's Rights Convention, she gave her "Ain't I a Woman?" speech. As you read her speech, feel the power of her story, her use of rhetorical figures and her passion.

"That man over there says that women need to be helped into carriages, and lifted over ditches, and to have the best place everywhere. Nobody ever helps me into carriages, or over mud puddles, or gives me any best place! And ain't I a woman? Look at me! Look at my arm! I have plowed, and planted, and gathered into barns, and no man could head me! And ain't I a woman? I could work as much and eat as much as a man – when I could get it – and bear the lash as well! And ain't I a woman? I have borne thirteen children, and seen most all sold off to slavery, and when I cried out with my mother's grief, none but Jesus heard me! And ain't I woman?"

I suspect that for the women at the Convention that day, Sojourner Truth's speech was a shared experience.

Chapter 9

Catalyst Number 4: Your Delivery

Nervousness and the Two P's

"According to most studies, people's number one fear is public speaking. Number two is death. Death is number two. Does that sound right? This means to the average person, if you go to a funeral, you're better off in the casket than doing the eulogy."

—Jerry Seinfeld

If you would rather be in the casket, have hope. Here is the cure. Nervousness is cured by the two P's, Preparation and Practice.

Preparation

Your preparation is composed of all of the work you will have done in the process of writing your sermon, not only in the five steps, but in your revisions and sleeping on it. By the time you get to practice, you have a secure grasp on what you are going to say.

Practice

"(The speech) is most worth listening to which has been carefully prepared in private and tried on plaster cast, or an empty chair, or any other appreciative object that will keep quiet until the speaker has got his matter and his delivery limbered up so that they will seem impromptu to an audience....in order to do an impromptu speech as it should be done you have to indicate the places for the pauses and hesitation."

—Mark Twain

After Mark Twain lost much of his fortune in bad investments, he supported himself by traveling around the world giving humorous speeches. He was good at it, received positive reviews and drew large audiences. He wrote his talks in full, marked them "to indicate the places for the pauses and hesitation", practiced them "...in private...on plaster cast, or an empty chair...until (he) ...got his matter and his delivery limbered up so that they will seem impromptu to an audience...", but he delivered them from memory.

Twain had an advantage over the preacher. He wrote his talk, memorized it and delivered it over and over around the world. A Sunday preacher has one week to write, practice, and deliver a sermon, and then start all over on Monday. Twain got paid better too.

"When I don't practice one day, I can tell the difference. When I don't practice two days, my wife can tell the difference. When I don't practice for three days, anyone can tell the difference."

—Arthur Rubinstein

When the producers of Broadway shows have a new show, they first have the actors rehearse their parts, over and over. Then to try it out, they open in New Haven. They watch the audience's reactions, rewrite the script, and the actors rehearse it again. Only after they have it right do they open on Broadway. The professionals know the value of rehearsal. They have too much of themselves and their backers' money invested in their performance to leave success to chance.

"In my seventeen years of preparing, teaching, and coaching presentations and public speeches ranging from client sales pitches to campaign kick-offs and State of the Union addresses, I have seen more speeches fail from lack of rehearsal than any other single problem."

—Nick Morgan [1]

If the first time you hear your sermon aloud is when you deliver it to your listeners, you will have just made a serious mistake. Morgan recommends you rehearse at least three times. That's the minimum. More is better, and sleep on it.

Mark Twain practiced "...on an empty chair." You have an advantage over Twain – the digital recorder. After marking up your text for pauses and inflection, you can practice, listen, and change your delivery. Listen for your passion.

Professional speech trainers also use TV cameras to let speakers see themselves as other see them. TV taping is especially useful in practicing pauses; even three seconds will wake up a dozing listener. Taping also shows nervous ticks, gestures and wooden body language that distract from an otherwise well-prepared sermon. You probably don't have the time to use this regularly, but as you try to improve your delivery skills, you might take advantage of this technology. Even occasionally self-recording your sermon as you practice will improve your delivery. A few dollars spent on a small, inexpensive recorder is a good investment.

As you practice your sermon, if you find a sentence difficult to remember, that might be a red flag that the sentence needs to be rewritten. If you use a compound sentence, imitate the professional radio speakers by pausing slightly at the conjunction. Your slight pause signals your listeners you are adding another idea.

Body Language

"When I hear a man preach, I like to see him act as if he were fighting bees."

—Abraham Lincoln

You deliver your sermon in two languages, verbal and body, and you need to be fluent in both.

"It isn't what I do, but how I do it. It isn't what I say, but how I say it, and how I look when I do it and say it."

—Mae West

When your verbal language and your body language are delivering two different messages, your listeners become unsure which is your real message. They instinctively suspect that your body language might be the real you, not your verbal language.

"When the eyes say one thing, and the tongue another, a practiced man relies on the language of the first."

—Ralph Waldo Emerson

How then to make sure your verbal language and your body language are delivering the same message? I believe the greatest force to insuring your verbal and body languages speak together is your passion. If your passion is real, if you feel it, and if you allow it to be seen and felt by your listeners, your body language will be authentic. It will deliver the same message as your verbal language, and your listeners will believe you.

However, just as we studied sentences and paragraphs, we should also study the basics of body language. If you have written your sermon so that it can become a shared experience, then it has a cycle of emotion within it. At times the emotional level is low, then rises and then falls. Your body language should correspond to that movement.

Body language has two components, stillness and movement. Stillness is similar to the pause in speaking. It creates a moment of calm and tells your listeners that you are comfortable and at ease with yourself. Your listeners can then relax and are better able to listen. It also allows you to establish a central reference position from which you gesture and move and to which you return.

If you feel comfortable leaving the pulpit, stand up straight in front of your listeners and face them squarely with your feet about your shoulder width apart. This is your central reference position. Pause slightly before speaking and remain in that place for at least thirty seconds to a minute. A good moment to move is when you transition to another idea (new paragraph), and then remain in the next place for at least thirty seconds to a minute.

As you sense a rising emotional level in your talk, lean forward slightly and move closer. As the level falls, you can move back to signal that a cooler moment has arrived. The "show" story with its higher emotional level is a time to move closer; then move back to continue. Another "show" story, parallel construction or repetition will raise the emotional level again. Your body language and movements should be consistent with the rising and falling emotional levels. You need to be aware of these cycles and move with them.

When we talk to another person or a few persons and become enthusiastic or emotional about what we are saying, we learn forward. We may even move closer into their personal space. Our facial expression reflects our animation. With our body gestures and movement, we reinforce the intimacy and emotion of the moment. The same is true when speaking to larger groups.

However, your gestures when you preach need to be different from when you talk in ordinary conversation. When you talk with a friend or a few persons in a small space, your gestures tend to be from the wrist or your lower arm. When you talk to many people in a large space, small gestures get lost. Raise your arms and gesture from your shoulders so they can be seen. If you are speaking outside of the pulpit and using 5" by 7" cards, feel free to gesture with them. Your listeners will see you are prepared and will appreciate it.

Eye contact helps you hold your listeners. Divide your audience into four or five sectors. Keep eye contact with each sector for five or six seconds and then move randomly to another sector. As you glance around, keep your chin level. If you raise it, your listeners will get the impression you are looking down at them.

Throughout this book and especially in Chapter 7 on rhetorical figures, you have read selections from the speeches of some of history's greatest orators. You might have heard and seen some of them in movies or video clips and learned how great orators deliver their speeches. You can learn body language in the same way and I will recommend some masters of body language for you to watch.

Masters of Body Language
Cary Grant is regarded by many film critics as one of the best – some say the best – kinetic actor in the history of films.[2] Grant, an acrobat and mime in his early career, mastered the craft of

telling the story not just with his words but with his body. Watch him dominate a scene with his small and large movements. Give yourself a treat and learn at the same time by watching him in "His Girl Friday" (1940), "The Philadelphia Story" (1940) or "North by Northwest" (1956).

Modern actors in the same tradition of kinetic acting include Jodie Foster, Denzel Washington, Sean Penn, Bill Murray and Cate Blanchett. As you watch these kinetic actors, see how the human body speaks its own language, sometimes more powerfully than the words the actor speaks. Some of the body language of these actors will not be suitable for preaching but by studying them, you will see the range of possibilities, and by imitating them, expand your body language vocabulary.

Unlike film actors, professional dancers speak to their audiences only with body language. Two of the greatest modern dancers and a great choreographer said this about one of their own: "...he simply was the greatest, most imaginative dancer of our time..."(Rudolf Nureyev); "He gives us a complex because he's too perfect..."(Mikail Baryshnikov); "He is the most interesting, the most elegant dancer of our time."(George Balanchine). The object of their admiration: Fred Astaire. After he created a dance routine, Astaire obsessively practiced it over and over, sometimes over fifty times. In her autobiography, Ginger Rogers, his dance partner, wrote that before filming, they practiced their dance routines eight hours a day for six weeks.[3] Baryshnikov said of Astaire, "He's a genius." If he were still alive, Astaire might disagree and quote Thomas Edison, "Genius is one percent inspiration, ninety-nine percent perspiration." Astaire knew that the body language of dancing required hard, physical work, but look at what those hard, sweaty practices produced – elegant dance routines that appeared effortless.

Astaire's example can help you. You must practice not only the verbal language of your sermons but also their demanding, body language. However, your hard work will be rewarded. You will deliver dynamic sermons and make them appear effortless.

I offer you these reminders and additional suggestions. Use your body language to take advantage of the first place of emphasis, your Introduction. These first two to three minutes are your opportunity to grab their attention. State your main idea and hook. If you have structured these two points well, they may immediately raise the emotional level. Pause slightly to let your words and gestures sink in. After that, get to your "show" story as soon as possible and move with the rising emotional level.

Research has shown that when teachers wait at least three seconds after asking questions, students' answers improve. Do not be afraid of silence. Your listeners need time to hear and absorb what you just said. Pauses also give emphasis to the ideas immediately before and after them. Use pauses for the ideas you want to emphasize.

"The right word may be effective, but no word was ever as effective as a rightly timed pause."
—Mark Twain

If you suspect that your body language is not as expressive as it could be, you might try this exercise once or twice. Lock the church where you preach. Then, safe from curious eyes in the security of the locked church, explore a more kinetic style of preaching. As you practice, concentrate on your body language as you speak, even exaggerate it to break through any inhibitions you might have. Coordinate your movements with the emotional level of your message. You can invite a friend to give you feedback.

Preaching Clearly

"Speak the speech, I pray you, as I pronounced it to you, trippingly on the tongue."
—Hamlet, Act 3, Scene 2

Vocal coaches tell us that almost everyone has some speaking characteristics that lessen the clearness of their words. So how do you speak your sermons so they are clear and understandable? To find the answers, we turn to phonology and vocal expression.

Phonology

Phonology, which is almost as exciting as diagramming sentences, is the study of sounds in languages. Phonology tells us that English is a stress-timed language in which the sounds of some syllables are short, some long, and the stress is placed on the important (strong) syllables and words. Less stress is placed on the less important (weak) syllables and words. The stressed words are usually the nouns, verbs, adjectives and adverbs. The less stressed are the conjunctions, pronouns, prepositions, and articles. These get "squeezed" between the strong syllables and words. The result is a recurring, irregular pattern that gives English its rhythm, its musicality, and makes it clear and easy to understand.

The importance of speaking English with the stresses can be appreciated when listening to some speakers of syllable-timed languages, for example, Indian, Japanese and Indonesian. Syllable-timed languages give each syllable the same amount of stress at a steady rate as the others. When those speakers have not mastered the irregular stress-timing of English, their conversations can be difficult to understand. Speaking English with the stresses is essential to making it understandable.

Even if English is your first language, you want to be certain you are taking full advantage of the rhythm and stresses of

English. To do this, I believe the most practical advice is for you to read your sentences aloud, listening for the rhythm. You are tuning your ear to hear the rhythm, the music.

When you speak with that rhythm, your listeners will hear the musicality of your speech. You might consider your voice a musical instrument that plays the music. How you use your voice is called your vocal expression.

Your Vocal Expression

Together with your passion, body language, and stress-timed English, you can add life to your sermon by your vocal expression. Without good vocal expression, your voice will sound flat and lifeless. Vocal expression consists of the pitch and volume of your voice, and the pace of your words. To preach well, you must control all three components of vocal expression.

Pitch:

Your vocal pitch, the lowness or highness of your voice, is similar to the scale of a piano keyboard. You probably have a two-octave range. Within that, you have your habitual pitch, the note your use most frequently, and your optimal pitch, the note at which your voice sounds best. Most speakers' optimal pitch falls within the lower half of their range. Because your listeners will be more receptive to your optimal pitch, you want to make that your habitual pitch.

Volume:

Even with the advantages of today's sound systems, you need to control the loudness or softness of your words and sentences for emphasis and to hold your listeners' attention.

Pace:

You set your pace by how quickly or slowly you speak your

sentences, how long you take to say a word, and how long is the silence you insert between your words, phrases and sentences.

You might consider following the example of professional actors and public speakers who work with voice coaches to raise the performance of their vocal expression. Before Margaret Thatcher's rise to prominence in British politics, her voice had been described as "shrill." Following the advice of Sir Lawrence Olivier, she worked with a vocal coach. He helped her lower her voice and slow her pace. You can hear the before and after results if you search on the Internet for: "Margaret Thatcher Voice." A few dollars and some time with a vocal coach could improve your vocal expression. When you combine your vocal expression with your stress-timed speaking, the result will be a clear, understandable sermon.

PRACTICE

Practice at least part of your next sermon aloud concentrating on your rhythm and vocal expression. Practice all future sermons at least three times.

Part Three

Growing as a Preacher

Alvin Toffler said: "The illiterate of the twenty-first century will not be those who cannot read and write, but those who cannot learn, unlearn, and relearn." I am now seventy-nine years old and during the sixty years since I was nineteen, I have learned, unlearned, and relearned more than I had planned. Some was voluntary, and some was forced upon me by circumstances. Voluntary is better. In Part Three, I will offer you some suggestions for you to unlearn and relearn. Please consider them. You will grow and preach better.

Chapter 10

Feedback from the Pews and Action Plan

"Do not seek praise. Seek criticism."
—Paul Arden[1]

In the school where I taught business writing for adults, the other instructors and I taught classes on contract, and each new class was a new contract. At the conclusion of every class, the participants filled out evaluation forms, rating me and the class. When the last person left the room, I immediately read their ratings and comments. It was a moment of truth. Once a year, I received a print-out giving the average of my ratings for the year. It was listed with the averages of the other instructors with their names deleted. The list began with the highest ratings and descended to the lowest. It told me where I stood in relation to the other instructors. With the printout came a letter which thanked me for my service, explained the printout, and then reminded me that if my ratings did not continue to meet a minimum rating level, I should not expect to receive any contracts in the future. Not subtle, but effective.

No one motivates someone else. Our motivation comes from within us, but immediate, honest and specific feedback from others on our performance can activate our desire to do better. If a person shakes a preacher's hand and says "That was a good sermon", it will make him feel good, but it is not helpful feedback. He doesn't know why it was good. But if someone else says "You point about …will help me. I'm going to do…because of it", he knows he got across his main idea and his "Call to

Action." Better yet, if someone says "I didn't understand your point about...," he knows he needed to have explained it better. That feedback is helpful because it is immediate, honest and specific, and the preacher is more likely to learn from it and improve his explanations in the future.

A friend told me about a priest who had said that he thanked God for having given him the gift of giving good, impromptu sermons. My friend said that the parishioners agreed that the priest was the worst preacher they had ever heard. Sadly both he and his listeners were losers in the transaction. The priest, who wanted to preach the Gospel well and had given his life to do so, was unaware he did it so poorly, and his listeners, who had come to be fed, went away hungry.

Chris Chatteris, S.J., writing about feedback and preaching, wrote: "We live in a world in which feedback is routine and is built into most forms of communication. Politicians, teachers, journalists and other communicators expect and welcome feedback. The maintenance and development of professional standards demands such feedback."[2]

> "Candor is a compliment; it implies equality. It's how friends talk."
>
> —Peggy Noonan

That old sage George Burns observed that vaudeville gave inexperienced performers "somewhere they could be bad." Unfortunately, churches do not have a vaudeville circuit for their new performers. The closest they have for an inexperienced preacher to be bad are seminary homiletics classes and the first assignment. Accept it: All inexperienced performers, preachers included, are bad or close to bad. The vaudeville performers who listened to their audiences, unlearned what was not working, relearned, and changed their acts, became successful.

"Failure gave me an inner security that I had never attained by passing examinations. Failure taught me things about myself that I could have learned no other way."

—J.K. Rowling[3]

My father had a saying: "Some people have ten years of experience; some have one year of experience, ten times." If you want to avoid having one year of experience, ten times but instead have ten years of learning experience to reach Mastery as a preacher, you need feedback. Even if your people are reluctant to give you immediate, honest and specific feedback, you must insist. You need it for them and for yourself. Feedback sometimes is painful, but it will help you grow and become better.

"The things which hurt, instruct."

—Benjamin Franklin

Lessening the Pain of Feedback

Feedback does not have to hurt. Those who give feedback can lessen any pain by making the feedback specific. Specific feedback focuses on problems in the sermon, not in the preacher. Even feedback on delivery, if specific, can be objective and not personal. However, those who give specific feedback need to have knowledge of the structure and techniques of a good sermon. You can either recruit people who have this knowledge or train them using the information in this book.

You might begin your search for feedback by placing some 3" x 5" index cards and pencils in the pews. After your sermon, tell your listeners that they might find a card and pencil near them. Ask them to write in one sentence what they thought was the main idea of your sermon and hand them in as they leave. You will get immediate, honest and specific feedback, and you will have taken your first step toward getting feedback.

> "Feedback is the breakfast of champions."
> —Ken Blanchard

When you are ready to ask for more comprehensive feedback, you will find **"Feedback Suggestions"** in the Appendices. You can give them to a preaching committee which Chatteris suggests and meet with them to get their feedback.

The Seminary Department of the National Catholic Educational Association has created a "Rating Form for Homily." They will e-mail you a copy if you contact them at: www.seminary@ncea.org.

PRACTICE

Seek feedback from a committee.

Action Plan

> "We learn to do something by doing it. There is no other way."
> —John Holt

If you decide you want to use some of the techniques in this book, you might want to develop an action plan. Because there's so much to master, I suggest you start with the techniques which will give you most returns right away. Then move on to other techniques.

The amount of knowledge and number of skill described in this book may seem to be overwhelming. However, learning new knowledge and skills is a gradual process for everyone, earned by practice, and lasting a lifetime. Be patient with yourself. Stay with your action plan and you will learn, grow, and become a better preacher.

Most Returns Quickly

Purpose; write it in a short, declarative sentence.

One Main Idea; write it in a short, declarative sentence.

Those Other Great Ideas (the distractions); delete them

Your "Call to Action"; make sure it flows from your purpose and main idea.

Sharpen the focus.

Good Returns with More Time

The "Hook"; write it in the Introduction.

Declarative sentences

Verbs

Write your Introduction and Conclusion.

Review and revise for emphasis.

Good Returns with More Effective Use of Your Time

Follow the Five Step Process of Writing a Sermon and sleep on it.

Write for the female and male tendency brains.

Keep a pad and pen by your bed to capture your "sleep on it" ideas.

Considerably Better Returns with More Time Invested

Recruit a sermon preparation group.

Schedule your preparation and three practices of your sermon over at least two or three days. Include practice of your body language. **Note:** You might want to move your three practices to the top of your Action Plan since they are so important to the success of your sermon.

Good Returns with More Writing and Revision Time

Write "show" stories when you experience or remember them and file them. Try to use one in every sermon.

Use rhetorical figures starting with parallelism.

Potential for Great Returns and Rewards

Identify and schedule your vital 20% tasks to produce your 80% results.

Pick whichever of the remaining techniques you want to master.

Read a book on preaching.

Part Four

Conducting Retreats and Days of Recollection

Silence is the soul of a retreat but sometimes retreatants might benefit from discussing their progress with the others. Guided group and sub-group discussions will allow them to do that. For over forty years I have facilitated group discussions and have picked up a few tricks along the way. I share them with you in Part Four.

Chapter 11

Group Facilitation Suggestions for Retreat Masters

As *a preacher during a retreat or day of recollection*, you have two advantages that the Sunday preacher does not enjoy. First, because you will usually speak at least two or three times, you can explore your theme in greater depth and breath. Second, you can involve your group in exploring the theme together. You can create a process in which your group can listen to your message, meditate in silence and then as a group discuss their thoughts and reactions

Group participation allows your listeners to process the information you give them in your sermon by discussing it among themselves. They can explore its meaning, its relevance and application to their lives and own their conclusions. Discussion will allow them to do that.

In Chapter 4, I described working with a homily preparation group and recommended the preacher not facilitate the meeting, but sit with the group, and ask a facilitator to lead the discussion. That is because the purpose of that kind of a short meeting is to produce insights (a product) which the preacher will use that week. By sitting with the group, the preacher can follow the process, comment as needed, and listen for the insights which will become the content of the homily. However, the purpose of your discussion is not production of a product. Its purpose is to facilitate a dialogue among the group members, and in the process, share insights that help all grow more than they would working individually. As the retreat leader, you are part of this dialogue so it is appropriate for you to guide the discussion.

Two techniques, guided group discussions and sub-group discussions, are the usual methods of structuring the process. In guided group discussion, you ask prepared questions of the entire group and you facilitate the discussion. In sub-group discussions, you separate the group into sub-groups and give them your prepared questions. They discuss them in sub-groups, usually from four to six people, and they report their thoughts back to the entire group.

The advantages of guided group discussions are they take less time than sub-group discussions and everyone hears the same insights. Their disadvantage is that many people can become just listeners and do not participate. They can become detached from the dialogue. The advantage of sub-group discussion is that everyone has the opportunity to participate and "own" the resolution. The disadvantage is it takes considerably more time.

Preparation

When you decide to include group discussions in your retreat or day of recollection, write out your questions carefully. You do not want questions that are so open-ended that your listeners will not know where to begin and you do not want questions that are so close-ended that the only responses are "yes," "no" or their equivalents. If you are talking to a group of women about prayer, an example of a slightly closed question might be: "How can you find opportunities for prayer in your busy day?" If you are using sub-groups, you can tell them they have fifteen minutes for their group discussions and five minutes for reporting out.

Facilitating the Discussions

A frequent problem in guided group discussions occurs when someone begins to monopolize the discussion by speaking up again and again. You can use your body language to prevent or at least minimize that. As you move away from that person, move to the people on the other side of the group and, by looking at them, encourage them to speak. If someone does speak, encourage her further by a "thank you; that's a good point". Once the group sees you welcome different points of view, they will begin to speak up. Continue to encourage them with your body language and your words.

Because the retreatants' responses are the fruit of their prayers, meditations and discussions, you want to record their progress. Facilitating a group discussion is a full-time job, so I recommend you get someone else, not a member of the group, to act as recorder. That will leave you free to pay attention to the group.

Your recorder will need at least one flip-chart with a stand, black and colored markers and masking tape. As a page is filled, the recorder will rip it off and tape it to a wall so everyone can see it. Continue the process until finished. This will focus everyone on the discussion as it progresses. Record everyone's contribution so they know they have been heard. The group will need help organizing and seeing a pattern in their thoughts. I suggest you use the breaks to study them to see if you see any patterns. When the discussions reach a stage of completion, you can ask the members if they see any patterns, "ideas that go together." You can use different colored markers to connect the ideas as they see them. Over a two or more day retreat, the pages will serve as a record of their progress. Leave the pages taped to the walls until the end of the retreat. You can use them as a quick review of what the group has accomplished.

When you ask your questions, read them exactly as you have written them. One incorrect word can move their discussions in a direction where you do not want to go. Ask only one question at a time. If you want to ask a follow-up question, hold it until they have reported out and then ask it as a guided-group question. In reporting out, make sure the first group doesn't give all the answers and leave everyone else to say "We had the same ideas." Take one response from each group and keep going around until no one has any more to add.

If someone asks you a question for which you don't have an answer, you have a few options. If it is a factual question, admit you don't know but you will find out and get back to her. If it is a question with gray areas that you know you need time to consider, you can ask for clarification: "Can you be more specific?" Rephrasing the question might frame it so you can get a handle on it. You can also say that question has gray areas to it and ask the group what they think about it. Frequently the group can help you by drawing upon their life experiences.

If someone asks a question that will take the group in another direction, you have two choices. You can allow the group to discuss it keeping in mind you will have to bring the group back to the main idea. You second choice is to put the question in a storage bin. Print BIN on a sheet of paper taped to the wall and ask if you can put the question in the BIN and return to it later. When this happens, time management becomes an issue so you will have to shorten some discussions.

The Room and Seating

Seating arrangements are important and usually fall into one of two formats. The first is designed for guided group discussion with everyone sitting in a semi-circle, facing you and each other. The second format is in small circles or at tables. This format is designed for sub-group discussions but can also be used for guided group discussion. I prefer this format because of its flexibility.

Make sure the room and seating work for you and not against you. If you will be speaking in a room you are unfamiliar with, make sure it and the seating arrangements are what you want. Do not be bashful about asking for changes in the seating arrangements. Bad seating arrangements can destroy group interaction and make you feel like you are dragging a dead elephant all day.

Try to get a room with natural light, especially if you will be together for two or more days. The lack of natural light affects the mood and even the energy level of groups. If windows are directly behind you, change the seating so the lighting comes from the side or rear.

Friends who come to days of recollection usually sit together and will continue to sit together in sub-groups unless you separate them. If you separate them, they will be more likely to talk more freely and will gain more from the different perspectives. Ignore my suggestion if you sense it will create a negative reaction. If you decide to move them, first explain that you want everyone to meet new friends and get the benefit of their experiences. To separate them, decide how many groups you want, then have them count-off by those numbers and assign them to groups by those numbers.

The Ice-Breaker

I have found in my training classes that helping people get to know each other at the beginning of a class always helps them work together better and learn more. I first tell them they are going to meet some interesting people and possibly make some new friends. Then I ask them to give their names and where they are from. If the group is not too large, you could add another question or two that you feel are appropriate and would help them get to know each other. I begin the introductions by telling them something about myself and then let them speak whenever they are ready. I encourage them with my body language to speak in random order because a set order makes some people nervous.

Finally, remember feedback. It will help you become better.

Chapter 12

Conclusion

"We are all apprentices in a craft where no one ever becomes a master."
—Ernest Hemingway

The craft techniques in this book may challenge you to change how you prepare, write and deliver your sermons. If you decide to make those changes, recognize your first attempts might feel uncomfortable. Like a basketball player who has always dribbled with the right hand and now must learn to dribble with the left, you will feel awkward and may not do well in your first efforts. But like the basketball player, with practice you will develop new skills, learn the crafts and perform better than before. As John Holt, an educator, said: "We learn to do something by doing it. There is no other way." You might never be satisfied with your performance but as Hemingway reminds us, no one becomes a master of these crafts. Nevertheless, no craft on earth is more noble or worthy of your efforts.

When you preach, you join a line stretching back over two-thousand years of those who have proclaimed the Good News that "…God so loved the world that he gave his only Son, that whoever believes in him should not perish but have eternal life." (John 3:16) You have accepted a glorious calling. It is a difficult and challenging task but your listeners will appreciate and welcome your preaching.

We need you and the Word you proclaim. You are a gift, a grace to us.

Acknowledgments

To my good friends who encouraged me and graciously gave me immediate, honest and specific feedback on my drafts, my sincere appreciation. They will notice that I did not accept all of their suggestions which means I alone am responsible for the errors and lapses in sound judgment.

My reviewers and contributors were: Father Ed Brady, Sister Sally Butler, O.P., Hugh Clear, Mary Clear, Joe Dougherty, Sister Karen Doyle, SSJ, Bill Duncan, Dick Fraser, John Kaseta, Frank Lawlor, Father Larry Madden, S.J. (May 18, 1933-June 8, 2011), Father Richard Martin, and Jim McDaniel.

Index

Appendices

The Process of Writing a Sermon

Review feedback from previous sermons.

Pray and read the scriptures.

Meet with the sermon preparation group.

Identify your primary purpose and your secondary purpose, if you have one.

Identify the one, main idea.

Identify the "Call to Action."

Brainstorm ideas. Include ideas suitable for systemic and relational development for the male and female brain tendencies.

Eliminate those other great ideas.

Sharpen your focus.

Schedule your writing time on your calendar.

Sleep on it.

Organize your ideas.

Identify ideas you want to emphasize with rhetorical figures.

Create your "hook."

Write a "show" story.

Determine if you will use the Conclusion to repeat your main idea for emphasis along with your "Call for Action."

Write first draft.

Revise.

Mark up for pauses and body language.

Sleep on it.

Practice a minimum of three times (verbal and body language).

Sleep on it

Preach with passion.

Revision and Edit Checklist

Did you first write your one, main idea in a simple, declarative sentence?

Did you write your purpose (and secondary purpose)?

Do you have a main idea in the Introduction?

Do you have a "Hook" in the Introduction?

Have you deleted all distracting ideas or facts?

Have you narrowed the focus of your purpose and main idea?

Have you repeated the main idea in Conclusion?

Do you have a "Call to Action" in the Conclusion?

Have you written a "Show" story that is set up well and built with details?

SENTENCES

- Does each sentence have just one idea?
- Have you rewritten compound sentences into simple declarative sentences?

- Have you eliminated all but the absolutely essential dependent clauses?

- If you have dependent clauses, have you marked your text to remind yourself when to pause at the comma?

- Have you replaced your "to be" verbs with action verbs?

- Have you changed your passive verbs to active verbs?

- Have you changed your smothered verbs (nouns) into action verbs?

- Have you replaced weak verbs with strong action verbs?

- Have you deleted the adjectives and adverbs?

- Have you identified opportunities for parallelism and revised for it?

- Do your personal pronouns recognize your women listeners?

- Have you varied the length of your sentences?

Have you read your text aloud to test for conversational rhythm?

Feedback Suggestions

Hints for the Preaching Feedback Committee

Take notes as you listen to the sermon.

Prepare your feedback before the meeting. Try to phrase your observations as positive suggestions rather than as negative statements.

Meet as soon after the sermon as possible; memories fade.

Be specific.

Be honest.

Don't use a scale of 1 to 10; it does not give specific feedback and therefore is not helpful.

Content:
What was the preacher's main idea?

Did the preacher stay with the main idea through the entire sermon?

Did you become interested right at the beginning?

If yes, what was it the preacher said that got you interested?

What were you asked to do at the end of his sermon?

Was it too long/not long enough?

Were you bored? Why?

The "Shared Experience":
What did you feel as you listened today?

Did you hear a story that moved you?

If yes, what was its point?

Delivery:
What did the preacher's body language say to you?

Was the preacher's delivery conversational and varied or "preachy"?

Did you see, hear and feel the preacher's passion about the message? Did the preacher vary her/his inflection, pitch and volume or was her/his vocal expression flat?

Quotations

"Preach the Gospel at all times – if necessary, use words."
—St. Francis of Assisi

"A ship in a harbor is safe, but that is not what a ship is built for."
—Rear Admiral Grace Hopper

"The only difference between the saint and sinner is that every saint has a past, and every sinner has a future."

"Starvation, and not sin, is the parent of modern crime."
—Oscar Wilde

"When I was young, I admired clever people. Now that I am old, I admire kind people."
—Rabbi Abraham Joshua Heschel

"…Violence begets violence."
—Patrick V. Murphy
Police Commissioner, New York City, Detroit

"As long as war is regarded as wicked, it will always have its fascination. When it is looked upon as vulgar, it will cease to be popular."
—Oscar Wilde

"Unless we teach our children peace, someone else will teach them violence."

—Colman McCarthy

"The bible tells us to love our neighbors, and also to love our enemies; probably because they are generally the same people."

"The Christian ideal has not been tried and found wanting; it has been found difficult and left untried."

—Gilbert K. Chesterton

"When I feed the poor they call me a saint. When I ask why there are so many poor and hungry, the call me a Communist."

—Dom Helder Camara

"While we are free to choose our actions, we are not free to choose the consequences of our actions."

—Stephen Covey

"Courage is what it takes to stand up and speak; courage is also what it takes to sit down and listen."

—Winston Churchill

"Don't call me a saint. I don't want to be dismissed so easily."

"I firmly believe that our salvation depends on the poor."

"The true atheist is the one who denies God's image in the 'least of these'."

—Dorothy Day

"If I knew she was so close to death, I would have been kinder."

> (Spoken by a son in his eulogy
> at the funeral of his mother)
> —Father Dick Martin

"There can be unity where there is not uniformity."[1]

> —Martin Luther King

"Resentment is like drinking poison and then hoping it will kill your enemies."

> —Nelson Mandela

"There is the risk you cannot afford to take, [and] there is the risk you cannot afford not to take."

> —Peter Drucker

"Everyone is entitled to his own opinion. No one is entitled to his own facts."

> —Daniel Patrick Moynihan

"If everyone is thinking alike, someone isn't thinking."

> —General George S. Patton

"If knowledge alone could save us from sin, the salvation of the world would be easy work."

> —Agnes Repplier

"Nothing like a little chest pain to restore your faith."

> —Ray Romano

"All God's children are not beautiful. Most of God's children are, in fact, barely presentable."
—Fran Lebowitz

"Matthew 25 is my final exam."
—John Foster Magill
Educator

"We must change to remain the same."
—Ichiro Ozawa
Japanese political leader quoting from the 1963 Italian film *The Leopard*

"Working for God on earth may not pay much, but the retirement plan is out of this world!"
—Father John Dunne SJ

"You do not lead by hitting people over the head – that's assault, not leadership."

"Pull the string and it will follow where you wish. Push it, and it will go nowhere at all."
—Dwight D. Eisenhower

"The key to successful leadership today is influence, not authority."
—Kenneth Blanchard

"He was of the faith in the sense that the church he currently did not attend was Catholic."
—Kingsley Amis

True Show Stories

THE TWO FRIENDS

Two women had been friends for many years. One Sunday morning, one woman called her friend and said: "My husband died last night. Would you come over and be with me?" "Yes" her friend replied "but first, I have to go to Mass. Then I'll come over."

—Father Dick Martin

THE MEAN NUN

Some graduates of a large parish school in Brooklyn happened to meet years after they had graduated. They reminisced about how much they liked the Sisters who taught them but how they had a bad memory about a particular Sister. She always made Jimmy go into the cloakroom every morning even though he hadn't done anything bad. They disliked her for that. One of the graduates said that she had learned later that Jimmy's family was so poor he didn't have any breakfast before he came to school. The Sister cooked his breakfast every day, hid it in the cloakroom and sent Jimmy in there so he wouldn't be embarrassed in front of the other children.

—Father Ed Brady

SEEING WITH MY HEART

One of my precious memories as a little girl is visiting my Grandmother. My favorite moments were sitting on her lap with my head against her. There I curled up, peaceful and content, in her embrace. My Grandmother would touch my face and say to me over and over again, "You are so beautiful. You are so beautiful." I remember the touch of her hand and the sweetness of her voice in these tender moments.

Then one day I realized that my Grandmother was blind and that she could not see me and that she never had seen me. As she touched my face and said her precious words, I said to her, "But you can't see me, Mom Mom. You can't see me." And then she said something I have never forgotten. She softly whispered, "Oh, yes I can. I can see you with my heart." At that very moment, I knew there was another way of seeing. I whispered back, ""I want to see like you, Mom Mom, I want to see with my heart!" Today I continue to whisper my little prayer: *Mom Mom, please let me see like you. Please let me see with my heart.*

—Sister Karen Doyle, SSJ

PEACE BE WITH YOU

A recently ordained married deacon preached a homily during the Easter season on Jesus giving His peace when He appeared to His disciples. Later that week on his job managing the distribution of newspapers, one of his employees called in sick. He didn't have any backup men so he had to get in a truck and deliver them himself. He dreaded meeting a store owner who he knew frequently said he didn't get what he ordered, got more copies and then sold them on the side, making more money. Sure enough, the owner started complaining about his last order. The deacon was about to give him a piece of his mind when he remembered his homily. He took a breath and said: "Peace be with you." The owner stopped, looked at him and then said, "Well, peace be with you too." Their relationship changed from then on.

—John Kaseta

THE SLAVE

I was in the Blessed Sacrament Chapel when two women came in. One woman made a profound genuflection in front of the tabernacle, opened it and placed a host in a pyx. As they started to leave, I said: "I am a lot older than you and I remember when we couldn't even touch the Host. It's wonderful seeing you taking communion to the sick." The woman answered: "Yes, I feel so unworthy to touch the Host but I remind myself that even a slave can carry a king."

—Ed Reynolds

GRACE AT THE CHECK-OUT COUNTER

I headed to the check-out lines at our local discount grocery store anxious to get home and found three check-out counters open. I quickly picked the one with an empty conveyor belt where an old, white-haired, white woman appeared to be almost finished. The checker, a middle-aged African-American woman, waited while the old lady who I then realized was leaning on a cane, slowly counted her money. Then I saw all of her items were piled up past the check-out. As I watched the other lanes move, I started to get impatient. Then the check-out lady began to bag and load, item by item, everything into the old lady's cart. When she was finished, she went over to the old woman, put her arms around her and kissed her. "Have a happy mother's day" she said. When she came back to check me out, I said "You took good care of her". She said "We have to take care of each other". Then she turned, picked up a plastic bag and said "Look what she knitted for me". In the bag was an inexpensive, white, hand towel, and along one edge was an intricately crocheted border. She had been taking care of the old woman for years.

—Ed Reynolds

AN ORIGINAL SIN

When I was in the fifth grade in P.S. 31, my parents decided to transfer me to a Catholic school. One day my mother told me she would pick me up at lunchtime and take me to my new school. I had trouble paying attention in class that morning so I made a paper airplane. My seat was in the back of the class so I threw the plane down the aisle to the front. The teacher asked:

"Who threw that airplane?" Everyone turned and looked at me so I stood up. "Did you throw that plane?" "Yes" I said. "Apologize to the class." I remained silent. "Apologize to the class." More silence. "All right, you can stand in the hall until you are ready to apologize to the class." I walked out into the hall and saw that the clock said eleven o'clock. I stayed in the hall. My mother picked me up and I never apologized to the class.

—Ed Reynolds

BEYOND THE RAIL

When I was five years old, my parents lost my sister Nancy who was two years old to a mastoid infection. Her death affected my mother deeply so the following summer, my father sent us to Ireland to help her recover with the support of her mother and family. On the ship, my new friend Ian and I took full advantage of our freedom to explore. One day we walked to the front of the ship where the rail ended about forty feet from the bow. From there forward, there was no rail. I climbed through the rail, walked to the right, learned over the edge, and peered down at the Atlantic Ocean rushing by. I could see the side of the ship and the curve of the white water cut by the bow. I was hypnotized by the sight but then noticed that the ship's side and the bow's white water were slowly disappearing and the ocean was directly below me. The ship was heeling to the right and I began to pitch forward. My right arm shot out, and my hand hit the rail. I grabbed it. As I continued to fall forward, my grip held, and I swung around in an arc over the ocean until my body came around and hit the rail. I grabbed it with my left hand and hung there. Slowly I climbed back through the rail.

I did not tell my mother. Years later I realized that my mother would have lost two children within one year, my wife would have married another, and my children would never have been born – if my hand had not hit the rail.

—Ed Reynolds

Suggested Reading List on Preaching

An Introduction to the Homily. Robert Waznak, 1998, Liturgical Press

Craddock On The Craft of Preaching, Fred Craddock, 2011, Chalice Press, St. Louis, Missouri

Craddock Stories, Fred Craddock, 2001, Chalice Press, St. Louis, Missouri

Preaching, Fred Craddock, 1985, Abingdon Press, New York

Preaching Better: Practical Suggestions for Homilists, Ken Untener, 1999, Paulist Press

Preaching to the Hungers of the Heart: The Homily on the Feasts and within the Rites. James A. Wallace, 2002, Liturgical Press

Preaching the Just Word, Walter Burghardt, 1996, Yale University Press,

Two documents on preaching from the Catholic bishops that Catholic preachers should read and other Christian preachers might find helpful are:

Fulfilled In Your Hearing; The Homily in the Sunday Assembly, 1982, Bishops' Committee on Priestly Life and Ministry, United States Conference of Catholic Bishops, Washington, D.C. You can find the entire document at: http://www.usccb.org/plm/fiyh.shtml.

Preaching the Mystery of Faith: The Sunday Homily, November, 2012, United States Conference of Catholic Bishops

http://www.cathomiletics.org
This site provides links to many sources, Protestant and Catholic, for the study of homiletics.

Parallelism in Abraham Lincoln's Gettysburg Address
www.ccc.commnet.educ
- At the bottom of the column on the left side, click on "The Guide to Grammar and Writing"
- Select Word & Sentence Level
- Select Parallel structure
- In the middle of the box, click on "Abraham Lincoln's Gettysburg Address"
- Click on "OK"
- At the bottom of the page, click on "slide-show"
- Watch the slide show
- After the slide show, it will automatically go to a full-page copy of the Address
Courtesy of the Capital Community College, Hartford, CT 06103

Kinetic Acting:
For more information on kinetic acting, use a search engine and enter "A One-Man Movement" Sarah Kaufman. It will take you to the *Washington Post* and the article by Ms. Kaufman.

Notes

Chapter 1:

[1] Gabriel Garcia Marquez, Novelist, Nobel Prize for Literature, 1982

Chapter 2:

[1] Quote from pp. 60-1 [80 words] from KENNEDY by THEODORE C. SORENSEN. Copyright © 1965 by Theodore C. Sorensen; renewed © 1993 by Theodore C. Sorensen. Reprinted by permission of HarperCollins Publishers.

[2] *On Writing: a memoir of the craft*, Stephen King, 2000, Scribner, New York, N.Y. 10020, page 124

Chapter 3:

[1] Quotations from pp. 9, 33, 52-3, 162 [280 words] from BETWEEN HEAVEN AND MIRTH by JAMES MARTIN, SJ. Copyright © 2011 by James Martin, S.J. Reprinted by permission of HarperCollins Publishers.

Chapter 4:

[1] *Harvard Science*, Medicine + Health, July 2, 2002, "But only if you sleep on it", Matthew Walker, Assistant Professor of Psychology, Harvard Medical School

[2] "Wealth, Income, and Power", September 2005 (updated January 2011), Professor G. William Domhoff, Sociology Department, Universitiy of California at Santa Cruz.

[3] Robinson Professor of Public and International Affairs, George Mason University, and business columnist for the Washington Post

[4] *The Seattle Times*, April 11, 2012

[5] *Working the Room, How to move people to action through audience-centered speaking*, Nick Morgan, 2003, Harvard Business School Press, page 225; reprinted with permission.

[6] *The Essential Difference, The Truth about the Male & Female Brain*, Simon Baron-Cohen, 2003, Basic Books, A Member of the Perseus Books Group, pages 1, 3-4

[7] "Evidence for a Collective Intelligence Factor in the Performance of Human Groups", Anita Williams Woolley, Science, 29 October 2010

Chapter 5:

[1] Red Smith, sportswriter, Pulitzer Prize, 1976

[2] *Bird by bird: some instructions on writing and life*, Anne Lamott, 1994, Anchor Books, page 19; reprinted with permission.

[3] William Osler, MD, one of the founding professors at Johns Hopkins Hospital, has been called the "Father of modern medicine."

Chapter 6:

[1] *The Art of Acting*, Stella Adler, 2000, Applause Books, New York, N.Y., page 60

[2] *The Brain, A Very Short Introduction*, Michael O'Shea, 2005, Oxford University Press, page 88; "By permission of Oxford University Press"/"By permission of Oxford University Press, USA"

[3] O'Shea, Ibid, page 86

[4] *This Is Your Brain on Music, The Science of a Human Obsession*, Daniel J. Levitin, 2006, Penguin Group, 375 Hudson Street, New York, New York 10014, page 193; reprinted with permission.

[5] "The Secrets of Storytelling; Why We Love a Good Yarn", Jeremy Hsu, September 18, 2008, Scientific American Mind, Vol. 19, Issue 4

[6] *Crow and Weasel*, Barry Lopez, 1990, North Point Press, San Francisco, page 48; used with permission.

[7] Father Dick Martin, Pastor, Church of the Nativity, Burke, Virginia

[8] Marie Howe teaches at Sarah Lawrence College, New York University and Columbia University. She was named the New York State Poet (2012-2014)

[9] "The Star Market", from THE KINGDOM OF ORDINARY TIME by Marie Howe, Copyright © 2008 by Marie Howe. Used by permission of W.W.Norton & Company, Inc.

[10] De Niro was quoted by Dustin Hoffman on the Charlie Rose Show, January 28, 2013.

[11] Olivier was quoted by Dustin Hoffman on the Charlie Rose Show, January 28, 2013.

[12] Philip Seymour Hoffman, actor/director, and TS Media, Inc. The quote is from his appearance on the PBS show, "Tavis Smiley," September 22, 2010. Used with permission.

[13] Rabbi David Wolpe is the Rabbi, Sinai Temple, Los Angeles, California; reprinted with permission.

Chapter 7:

[1] Dr. Martin Luther King Jr., "I Have a Dream" speech; Reprinted by arrangement with the Heirs to the Estate of Martin

Luther King Jr, c/o Writers House as agent for the proprietor, New York, NY. Copyright 1963 Martin Luther King, Jr., copyright renewed 1991 Coretta Scott King
[2] President John F. Kennedy's inaugural address, January 20, 1961

Chapter 8:
[1] Dennis Wholey is the host of the TV show, "This Is America with Dennis Wholey."
[1] Morgan, ibid, page 26
[2] The Washington Post, A One-Man Movement (Cary Grant), Sarah Kaufman, January 11, 2009
[3] *Ginger, My Story*, 1991, Ginger Rogers, HarperCollins Publishers, 10 East 53rd Street, New York, NY, 10022, page 136

Chapter 10:
[1] *It's Not How Good You Are, It's How Good You Want to Be*, Paul Arden, 2003, Phaidon Press, New York, New York, page 26
[2] To read Chatteris's article and get his suggestions, go to: americamagazine.org, click on Archive, then May 25, 2009; reprinted with permission.
[3] Harvard Commencement Speech, 2008

Quotation:
[1] Ebony Magazine, June 1958

CPSIA information can be obtained at www.ICGtesting.com
Printed in the USA
LVOW10s2256161214

419198LV00014B/487/P